Simple Ways
to Access Your

Intuition
'On Demand'

John Living, Professional Engineer

'True Holy Love, Namaste'

"I see in you myself;   I recognize in you my image;
I will do my best to help you in your life for good intent,
Without harm or hurt to any."

The Holistic Intuition Society
www.in2it.ca

The Holistic Intuition Society

c/o Executive Secretary: John Living, Professional Engineer
RR# 1 S9 C6, Galiano Island, BC, V0N 1P0 Canada
Telephone (250)539-5807 Toll Free Canada & USA: 1-866-369-7464

Check the Society's web site for any changes: **www.in2it.ca**

For more books by John Living see:
www.in2it.ca/Books.htm

Intuition 'On Demand'

ISBN 978-0-9686323-3-8

Why be difficult, when
- with a little more effort,
You can be absolutely impossible

INDEX

About the Author

Teaching staff at Southend High School, the Royal Military Academy, Sandhurst, the School of Military Engineering, Chatham, and the Royal Military College of Science, Shrivenham, all attempted to give John Living an education.

He was one of the first officers commissioned by Her Majesty Queen Elizabeth II into the Corps of Royal Engineers, and is believed to have been the first British commander of a nuclear armed vessel - which is another long story !

Perhaps due to some mix-up, he was awarded an Honours Degree in Civil Engineering by London University, and has been a Royal Engineer, a Chartered Civil Engineer, and a Professional Engineer.

John has had experience in the Military, in Real Estate, as a Town Councilor, and has worked as an engineer as the Resident Engineer in charge of major projects, as a Consulting Engineer, as an Engineer in a major city, and in a senior position with a National Government.

Born in London, England, he has lived in Jamaica, and now resides in Canada - living in a cabin overlooking the golf course of Galiano Island, midway between Vancouver and Victoria in British Columbia, where he is watched by eagles, swallows, humming birds, deer, and golfers.

John is currently employed as the servant of two dogs, does Intuitive Healing work on the side, and writes in his spare time.

He can be seen wandering around looking rather lost, puffing a Peterson Pipe and wearing a Deerstalker Hat (like Sherlock Holmes), while he searches for clues as to the meaning of Life.

Failing to succeed is not failure;
Failure is not trying to succeed !

Introduction

Thank you for taking an interest in this book - I hope that you will find that it gives you a few good ideas of how you can access your 'Soul Senses' and your Intuition to improve your own life - and that of others.

I am an engineer - not trained as a literary person; so the style of this book is more akin to an instruction manual than a novel. I have tried not repeat myself too much, so to get the most out of this book you may have to read it more than once.

I believe that there is a Power greater than us, a Power that is benign and wants to help us; but there are a few big problems - often we are not aware of this help, we do not listen when help is offered, we fail to show our gratitude when such help is given - and we have given so much of our own power away to others.

It seems to me that this Power can do many things that we cannot do - especially in the non-physical realms. In the same way, often we can do things in the physical realm more easily than 'Upstairs' - my label for this Power.

When we work together with 'Upstairs' for the good of all creation, most things are possible ! But may take time to happen.

This is best accomplished when we regain the powers of our own that we have given away to, or had taken by, others. So much of what we do is governed by our beliefs - mostly things that we have been told or taught by others.

Often these were not for our own good, although that is what we were told - but for control. This includes what we were told by our parents, our religious leaders, our school authorities, and our governments.

In many of these cases, what we were told were the honestly held beliefs of others, who believed that they were doing good. But were such beliefs the real truth ?

Are we, as human beings, capable of understanding the real truth ? Many things are beyond our comprehension, and we may only be able to grasp a few of them. Imagine telling a person from a thousand years ago about electricity, radio, germs, or nuclear warfare.

My strongest belief is that we must keep an open mind. Hold the things that we have been told as if they were pieces of a jig-saw puzzle that we are trying to complete. We assemble groups of pieces, but when we try to fit those groups together there are mis-matches - so we have to re-assemble parts of these groups.

I have not yet got all my jig-saw pieces to give a complete finished picture - but perhaps the hints that I give in this book may help you to form your own picture better.

Remember that some of the pieces in my puzzle may not belong in yours - we all have our own puzzles to solve, and yours may already have pieces that belong to others, not you.

When working to make your puzzle be finished correctly, it is important to be working on a firm base - otherwise the pieces will keep falling apart.

Perhaps the strongest base to use is Love. Especially 'True Holy Love' - best described by 'Namaste':

> *"I see in you myself; I recognize in you my image;*
> *I will do my best to help you in your life for good intent.*
> *Without harm or hurt to any."*

The key here is not to help if harm would ensue to any life form - to help manifest only that which is beneficial to all.

Perhaps LIFE is given by 'Upstairs' in LOVE - and perhaps 'Upstairs' does not want worship - but help in creating and spreading more LOVE

If so, let 'LOVE' and 'LIFE' be interchangeable in all that you think, all that you do !

Remember, what you give out usually comes back to you, often more strongly and in different, unexpected ways.

That is my sermon - now let the lessons be read !

                             Namaste   *John*

*Intuition is **NOT** our sixth sense !*

Intuition uses all our senses to give the message !

Naturally, We ARE Intuitive !

Have you ever felt 'something is not right' - and, forewarned, avoided a problem ?

Have you met someone for the first time and felt something about them - and been correct ?

Have you lost something and then thought 'it is there' (in an unexpected place) and so looked and found it ?

Have you felt apprehensive before eating something, eaten it, and had a stomach ache ?

If any thing like this has happened to you, then you have been Intuitive.

We are all Intuitive to some degree - and can all improve our Intuitive abilities; and it helps to understand more about the Intuitive process, so that we can choose the method that suits us best.

A Simple Exercise

Stand up, and form a simple YES/NO question in your logical mind, such as *"Am I wearing clothes ?"*

Next, being sincere (as in prayer) ask your Heart this question and be aware of any slight body movements.

If you bent or swayed forward, the answer is YES ! A backwards movement would indicate NO.

Practice on a few more simple questions, such as:

"Am I over [or under] the age of XX years ?"
"Am I male [female] ?"
"Have I visited [a country ot city] in the last 20 years ?"
"Is my name [one of your correct names] [incorrect name] ?"
"Do I enjoy [favourite hobby/sport] ?"
"Do I regret any actions that I have made ?"
"Are there improvements that I can make to my life ?"

What is Intuition ?

Winston Churchill is understood to have said *"in truth, all people are offered help by their intuition - but most pick themselves up and escape as fast as possible".*

Those of us who accept this help become convinced that it is a 'Force for Good', and wish that it could be accessed 'On Demand'.

Guidance from 'The System' is a fair definition, 'The System' being the total environment in which we operate in life, including our memories, our sub-conscious self, our Guides, our 'Higher Self', and our 'Guardian Angels' and Deities as representatives of 'God' (or whatever labels we choose to use), and the total knowledge banks and information centres of 'All that Is' in the past, present, and (to some extent) the future.

In 'Awakening Osiris' - the beautiful and topical translation of the 'Egyptian Book of the Dead' by Normandi Ellis - it tells about the first human: Horus, the son of Osiris and Isis ...

"He was born out of death, carrier of his Fathers wisdom, he was the living emblem of Love. He was the Light triumphing over darkness, the first man, the miracle of nature - and he was followed by magic. A pair of hawks circled above him ... **They dropped two plumes which he placed on his forehead, two gifts that fell from the sky - Intuition and Love, gifts from the Goddesses - that he might walk towards Heaven and his Father, and never lose his way".**

Intuitive Examples

It is recognized that humans have five senses - seeing, hearing, feeling, tasting, and smelling. Many people have called Intuition our 'sixth sense'- having direct input into our conscious thoughts.

It is more correct to understand that Intuition is at a level above our senses, and uses them to get messages to us.

Usually we recognize our Intuition only when an especially important message is received such as not feeling 'good' about a person or situation, or we get an impulse to take a particular action.

There have been a number of well publicized cases when a person has felt that a particular flight or journey was 'not good' and so cancelled or changed their reservation - and avoided death or serious injury when their original plane or train crashed.

Mothers are well known to have special 'connections' to a baby - automatically knowing if their child is in trouble, and racing to prevent a tragedy.

Some notable investors who are most successful admit to relying heavily on their intuition, and revising their investments when they feel that that a stock is 'troubled'.

Scientists and inventors may get a sudden idea - and it often leads to a successful solution of the very problems that they have been concerning them.   Einstein has told that his understanding of relativity occurred in this way.

Perhaps the biggest difference between top executives is their attitude to Intuition - those who use it as a helpful indicator tend to be more successful.

Our Real Sixth Sense

In fact we do have a sixth physical sense, but most people are so accustomed to it that they overlook it as a separate sense - it is our sense of balance.

We have balance sensors associated with most of our joints - hence the skill of tightrope walkers, of steeplejacks who build high structures, and of waiters who carry loaded trays through crowded restaurants without spilling their loads.

They have developed a greater awareness of the 'feedback' from these receptors than most people; but we can all improve such awareness - and the first part of this is to realize that we do have this sixth sense, the sense of balancing.

When you asked your Heart the questions in our first experiment, you received an answer by a body movement; this was your Heart-Mind-Brain team working with your nervous-muscular system to give you a signal - by adjusting your 'balance system' so that your body swayed forward to indicate YES, or backward to indicate NO.

How does Intuition Operate ?

It seems that Intuition has three modes:

1. Forcing a message in some way if the matter is really important - and doing this even if the recipient is not normally open to Intuition.

2. Giving messages of various descriptions to people who are normally open to Intuition.

3. Responding to questions that are asked by those that actively seek the help of their Intuition.

In this book we are concerned with the third mode - that of asking questions and getting correct answers 'On Demand'.

Awareness is Most Important

The more that we are aware of our environment, the easier to note any changes in our perception. Seeing not just an object, but all the contouring, shading, and variations in colour (and carefully noting the surrounds and background) gives us a better appreciation of 'what we see'.

When we ask our Intuition for help on a subject, we can also define that 'all that we see' in the next few minutes has a meaning relating to the subject.

We will still perceive the same views as would have otherwise been seen, but our sight now may emphasize certain shapes, colours, contrasts, or even objects.

When ready, be fully aware of your environment, ask your question, and then note all the changes to your environment - a memory of a person or situation that comes to mind, a change of taste in your mouth, the shivers, a funny smell, hearing a noise that you did not notice before, or a picture flashing into your mind.

You may walk down the street and notice a particular colour, shape, or object; perhaps certain flowers in a garden 'call' to you; or your attention may focus on something in a shop window. Yes, all these things were there before, but your Intuition is now drawing your attention to them to 'get a message across'.

You seek guidance on a situation, and a memory of a person or a happening comes to mind - could your relationship with that person, the memory of how they behaved (to you or to others), or the outcome of that happening be an indication regarding your present situation ?

Laura Day, who has written a number of books on Intuition, suggests another way in her 'Practical Intuition': ask the question, and then check - How do I feel ? What am I thinking now ? What taste is in my mouth ? What am I smelling ? What am I seeing first when I close and then open my eyes ?

Also write down the first thing that comes to mind when you think of a place, person, colour, time, town, river, food, weapon, fear, memory, etc; you can write each of these on a card, and go through them to get immediate answers; do each one quickly - and if you do not get an answer then make one up !

Understanding Intuition

It pays to immediately record all your intuitive experiences. Often you will find a pattern that indicates the way that your intuition works.

Certain symbols seen (or persons popping into your mind) may have special meanings, even appearing in dreams.

By recording these, you may find the key to deciphering such meanings.

Then we have to 'make sense' of these impressions - a job fitting for the logical part of our thinking team !

It helps to ask for further clarification, and a thought may 'pop' into your mind.

That 'first thought' is probably from your Intuition, and should be taken seriously; any second thoughts are likely to be from your logical mind, and may best be disregarded.

This is probably because one's ego seems to operate from the logical part of the mind; being egoistic, it thinks that it 'knows it all' - and tries to imply that any other thought must be nonsense !

This would also explain why asking questions of your mind will tend to tell you the answers that you want to hear - by asking your Heart, you will be getting a more correct answer.

Knowledge Base

When you ask a question the answer can only be understood within the limits of your knowledge. The more knowledgeable that you are, the greater the range of contexts that can be used to give a true answer.

Imagine a nuclear physicist trying to explain sub-atomic particles to a class of young children, a scientist talking about television to people living in the Amazon jungle, or an astronaut telling of his trip to Europeans in the fifteenth century who believed in a flat earth.

You do not have to be a nuclear physicist to understand atomic theory, but you do have to understand the basic principles of chemistry and physics - and the more depth of knowledge, the more that can be understood.

We know about atoms, and can understand molecular chemistry. But have we seen an individual atom ?

We rely on what we can see and believe some of what we are told. This forms the contextual framework that we use in our own life.

We can see light, and the things that it illuminates; we know that they are real. Who has seen an X-ray or a radio wave ? We can observe an X-ray picture and listen to a radio - so we now know that they are real. But imagine trying to explain these energies to someone from a few centuries past !

Perhaps there are many more energies that we do not recognize, or do not understand. Our own reality is guided by our own belief system. If we have a fixed belief system then we cannot change.

Most of our belief system has been constructed from things that we have seen or been told - and what we were told may not be the real truth, only a belief that has been passed on.

It is important to keep an open mind, to accept that all that we are told is believed by others - but may not be correct. We can include (or exclude) things in our own belief system as we decide.

Having an open mind enables ourselves to grow, to increase our knowledge and understanding of all things.

Prophecies

One of the big problems with prophecies is that prophets who could see pictures of the future had to understand what they were shown, and then try to explain their prophecies in terms that their contemporaries could understand.

Nostradamus saw pictures of wars in the 20th century - he told of Hitler (as Hisler - the German way of writing ?) and was precise about the death of Mussolini.

He described a submarine periscope as 'the eye of a dog' and a helicopter as 'oars against the wind'.

Nostradamus was a brilliant prophet, but due to fear of persecution he scrambled the time lines, which makes most of his prophecies useless as forecasts tied to any period of years.

Mother Shipton, who lived in northern England about the same time, kept the sequence correct - and most of her prophecies up to date have come true; see web sites www.crystalinks.com/shipton.html and www.mothershiptonscave.com/main.htm to get a forecast for the near future.

Have you ever heard the phrase *"It's a bunch of malarkey"*? The Irish Church had St Malachy / Malarkey (1095-1148) (note spelling was not formalized in those days) who made a prophecy - he gave an identifier of each Pope to come in the future. For this and some other prophecies, see www.crystalinks.com/papalprophecies.html

Naturally the Church of Rome was not amused, doing its best to discredit the prophecy - even though the identifiers have proved correct in most cases. So any thing else which was discreditable was called *"a bunch of malarkey"*.

The last three elements of the prophecy (Pope John Paul II, his successor, and the end of the Church) are:

... **De Labore Solis** (Labour of the Sun) Pope John Paul II was born during a total eclipse of the sun.

... **De Gloria Olivae** (Glory of the Olive) the penultimate Pope. Pope Benedict - the colour olive is associated with the Benedictine Order.

... **Peter Romanus** (Peter of Rome) *"During the final persecution of the Holy Roman Church there will sit upon the throne Peter the Roman, who will pasture his flock in the midst of many tribulations. With these past, the city of the hills will be destroyed, and the awful judge will judge the peoples."*

Note that 'awful' is often used to describe something that is terrible (full of terror) or extremely bad; perhaps it also means 'full of awe' or 'to be held in awe, in high esteem'.

Many of the prophecies in religious books are probably correct, but told in language that could be understood at the time of writing, trying to describe what (at that time) was indescribable.

As shown above, the meaning of words has often changed with time; many works were passed down verbally, only to be in written form centuries later - and then translated into various languages.

Such translation often misses the nuances used in older times, and is subject to the bias of the translator who, for various reasons, may 'adjust' the context to conform with beliefs held.

Science and Religion

One of the major tragedies due to the extent of the authority throughout the western world of the Roman Catholic Church is the split between Science and Spirit. This is due to a battle between the 'flat earth people' and the 'roundheads'.

Although the wisdom of the East had always known that the earth was roundish and orbited the sun, in Europe the belief was that the world was flat - and that if you went too far you would fall off (which helped to explain losses of ships).

The Roman Catholic Church subscribed to the theory (actually their strong belief, not just a theory !) that the earth was the centre of the universe, and that all planets, suns, and stars revolved around the earth - in the heavens.

Young Galileo had got a telescope, and was using it to look at the stars - which were in the heavens, the domain of the Church ! And this dreadful fellow was telling everybody who would listen that the Church was wrong !

Of course, with the threat of eternal damnation and lesser penalties, not too many did listen. But there were enough to start a movement to check this new fangled idea - and soon the evidence became overwhelming. So much so that the Roman Catholic Church had to admit that Galileo was right (not, of course, that the Church was wrong).

Finally a deal was negotiated between the Church and these mad scientists - they could delve further into physical matters, so long as they did not poke their noses into anything spiritual.

All the European universities at that time (and for many succeeding centuries) were founded with close ties to the Church - and so this deal was enforced within these places of learning. If you wanted tenure, you 'toed the party line'.

This included supervising all research, so all became subject to 'proper scientific validation' - confined to the physical dimension.

Even today, if a scientist dares to explain things by associating them with the non-physical then he is subject to revile and his papers are not published. The 'peer review' system keeps present beliefs entrenched - changes could lower the prestige of the established leaders.

It is interesting to realize that many key inventions were made outside of university influence - Stephenson and his railway engine, the Wright brothers in flight, Edison and light bulbs, Marconi and radio waves, the Kirlians and auric photography, and many more.

Perhaps changes are now in progress; physicists delving into sub-atomic particles are finding that they are having to investigate other dimensions to explain their observations - including the now established fact that their observations and beliefs affect the outcome of experiments !

Other Dimensions

One such well known experiment is the splitting of a photon by an electron - reforming into 2 photons. Photons travel at the speed of light; when a photon is split, the two new photons are each traveling at the speed of light, but in opposite directions away from their original position.

A photon can be measured as a wave or as a particle. If either of the 'splits' is measured as a wave or as a particle, then it has been found that the other split can only be measured as the same wave or the same particle.

Somehow a message is passed from the first split to the second split *"I am measured as a wave (or particle)"* and determines the state for measurement of the second split. And this message is received almost instantaneously.

The relative speed between the two splits is twice the speed of light - so the message, the thought of 'how I am measured', must travel at many times the speed of physical light !

So to investigate sub-atomic physics requires an acceptance that there are other dimensions. Electrons are found to 'be there' and then 'not be there' - perhaps moving between dimensions.

Mathematicians, trying to build a mathematical model of the universe, have found that at least 10 dimensions are needed. In the physical world we are aware of four - length, width, height, and time.

It is possible that the missing dimensions have higher wave speeds - for electrons, for light, and for thoughts. Perhaps each dimension has an influence on all that is in those dimensions that operate at slower speeds - and that the reverse is also true.

Rupert Sheldrake suggests that we exist in 'metamorphic fields' where all that has ever occurred is in continual vibration as 'standing waves', which others have likened to a 'holographic universe'.

It is probable that our Intuition is our own link to such metamorphic fields (remember that this is just a label that we use for description) including the fields formed by the thought patterns of others.

Thoughts

When we have a thought, get a feeling, or express an emotion, we broadcast it to 'All that Is', as do all animals, reptiles, insects, and plants.

Perhaps the unimportant broadcasts are dissipated over time, but those that 'The System' considers to be noteworthy seem to be stored - added to 'The System's' store of knowledge or retained as memories in any stones or crystals affected.

A thought that is broadcast is like a pebble thrown into a pond - it sends ripples that travel the whole surface, perhaps meeting other ripples and changing to jointly form an interference pattern, similar to that used in a hologram.

We, and 'All that Is', receive these complicated interference patterns; from our interpretation of these interference patterns we formulate our own actions.

Thus each thought that we have (and broadcast) has a potential effect in the future, both our future and that of others.

Any thought, etc., that we broadcast is sent out as a symbol; my thought, if in English, is translated into a set of symbols; a Chinese speaking recipient gets the symbols, and his sub-conscious reacts; if considered to be important to his conscious self then the symbols are probably translated into his Chinese dialect.

Thus it is seen that language is not a barrier. Plants and animals also communicate using these same symbols, which helps to explain Cleve Backster's experiments.

Cleve Backster's Experiments

Some years ago the lie detector specialist Cleve Backster became interested in plants. He decided to test how long it took for water in a plant pot to reach the top leaf in a plant which was dry, so he attached a lie detector to the top leaf.

Backster was amazed to see that the lie detector indicated happiness as soon as it was attached, even though no water had been added.

He then wondered if the plant would give an unhappy signal if he set the leaf on fire - and was astounded that the plant gave that unhappy signal as soon as he had the thought ! This experiment has been well publicized both in books and on television.

Later, detectors connected to his plants in California were able to indicate his emotional state when he visited New York. In other experiments, detectors connected to blood samples have been shown to fluctuate with the emotional state of their donors when miles away, and continue to do so for a number of hours.

Dr Emoto's Crystals

Dr Masaru Emoto in Japan has spear-headed the investigation of water crystals subjected to various thoughts - that they hold the vibrational pattern of the thoughts.

When he took two samples of the same distilled water and wrote 'Hitler' on one and 'Mother Theresa' on the other, the crystal from the Hitler sample was distorted and even has a little picture of Hitler in the crystal - the one of Mother Theresa was beautifully formed.

He played different music to water as it crystallized - heavy metal and rock music caused mis-shapen crystals, while the music of Bach yielded well formed crystals.

Incredibly, when the water was from cultures of flower essences, the distinctive patterns of the flowers could be seen - their vibrationary patterns ! Read his book 'Message from Water' and see the web site:

www.life-enthusiast.com/twilight/research_emoto.htm

Crystals were formed from water taken from a large and polluted lake before and after a Japanese blessing service; they changed from being distorted to having a beautiful shape, matching the change observed in the lake itself.

About 70% of the weight of a human body is water; this helps to explain the changes in a human when subjected to various thoughts from other people - and your own thoughts.

The food that you eat also is mainly water, so Blessing what is consumed improves the beneficial value of the food - at very little cost !

Before Prayer   Fujiwara Dam   After Prayer

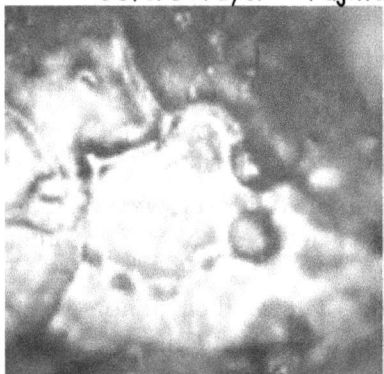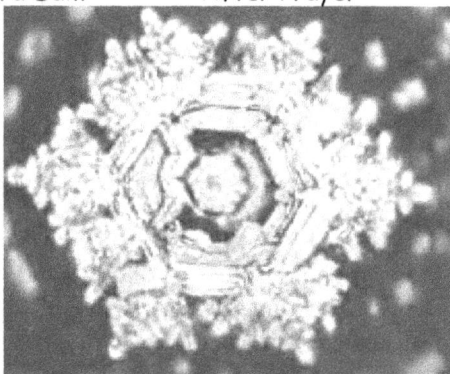

Dr Masaru Emoto   "Thank You"

The Human Being

We believe what we can see. When we see another human being we see their face, their clothes, and other parts of the body that are not hidden. We see movements and expressions which we can interpret as signals.

But our sight is limited to a small range of the electro-magnetic spectrum, which includes the colours of the rainbow; we cannot see infra red or ultra violet light, although the effects of light in these colours can be observed.

Some people can see more - and they report that our bodies are surrounded by auras, and that there are flows and patterns of different colours in the various parts of our auras.

Western medicine considers the body to be a bio-electro-chemical system, with various organs that can be dissected and sometimes exchanged, like using spare parts to repair an automobile or computer.

Eastern wisdom accepts that there are systems that cannot be seen, but are crucial to a person's health and well-being.

Both are correct - but the body is more than even the combination of these views. Life force is recognized as existing, but has never been examined; and many religions believe that we 'have a Soul' without being able to describe it completely.

Perhaps it is more correct to know that we are Souls that are having an experience in human bodies.

Ships of 'Being'

How can we describe ourselves ? Are we like ships sailing the oceans of existence ? If so, then our Conscious Self would be the Captain, leaving the routine running of our bodies to the officers and petty officers such as our sub-conscious, our glands and organs, our limbs, and our nervous, muscular, and other systems.

Our Heart, our ego, our sub-conscious, the logical and the intuitive parts of our thinking team - they are like the senior officers; very often they do not 'get on' with each other - or the Captain ! Perhaps they have been trying to get their viewpoint to the Captain without success, so are 'taking action' to get their message noticed, which may be disrupting the operation of our ship (causing sickness ?) and spoiling our voyage through life.

Each ship has a communications centre, which in our case may be the intuitive part of our thinking team, equipped with many radio receivers to listen to numerous broadcasts; but most of these do not concern the ship, or are of general interest.

Imagine the communications officer getting an enormous number of such messages; he has to decide which are important, and to whom they should be sent - and not many end up on the Captain's table. Perhaps the Captain has asked for information or help, and some of these messages may be to guide him, but unknown to the communications officer - so are not forwarded.

Some may be sent to the bridge, but the First Mate (the logical part of our thinking team) may not like them, think that they are not important, or try to deal with them himself - or putting his own 'twist' on the report to the Captain.

It seems that the main priority is to get the ship's crew to work together - in Peace, Harmony, and Love. Balancing the left and right sides of our brain is often meant as getting the logical and intuitive parts of our thinking team to be better 'team mates'.

Telling all parts of our Being that we love them and appreciate all that they do for us is similar to the Captain speaking to all the crew, to help get them all working together for the overall benefit of the ship. The help and co-operation of the Chief Petty Officer is critical - he leads the crew; perhaps we may recognize him as our Heart.

Having the ship in good order and the crew working well together helps us in stormy weather and when sailing in dangerous waters !

Often the ship sails to new ports, where customs and language differ; and we meet other vessels on the way. We may exchange energies with some, tell them about places we have visited, or let them know of any revisions to the charts used for navigation.

When we set sail we seldom know where we are going in life - we may have 'sealed orders' from pre-birth, or be pushed off course by storms or incorrect charts.

Some other ships may signal that they have messages or supplies for us, and others may be flying flags which tell us to beware.

Occasionally a ship may appear to be friendly, but turn out to be run by pirates; in such cases having good communications can help to get good guidance from the Admiralty - perhaps a friendly warship for protection, or even a flight of Angels overhead !

'Know Thyself'

Atoms form the cells of our bodies; a body which is alive has more than just atoms - it has a life force which has defied all scientific attempts to locate or define it, perhaps a Grand Form of Love.

'Atom' comes from the Greek language, and means the smallest possible particle that can exist: but today we know of many sub-atomic particles. The view of many physicists is that an atom is not even solid, but is mainly space - a tiny nucleus at the centre (like the sun) with electrons in orbit around (like planets).

Over one hundred years ago Leadbeater and Besant were able to describe the different atoms and their sub-atomic particles - the existence of these only being confirmed by scientists many years later when electron microscopes were developed. But what they described in 'Occult Chemistry' goes far beyond the facts so confirmed; they were able to see four layers of aura around every sub-atomic particle !

Perhaps these auras are made by very tiny 'Beings' - 'Baby Energies' - each of which can Feel, Love, Think, and Act to a limited degree. Perhaps they form 'All that Is' by doing different dances at selected frequencies of vibration.

The larger the concentration (and the greater the complexity of their organization) of these 'Beings' then the greater their potential ability to Feel, Love, Think, and Act.

If this be so, then it explains the old wisdom that 'We are All the Same' - made by 'dance teams' of the same 'baby energies' in various combinations of inter-related dances.

I may be incorrect in my understanding, but such a hypothesis goes a long way to explaining how plants and pets can communicate with humans and how memories can be retained in objects and used by many 'psychics' to give readings.

Auras and Chakras

There are many reports from people who are clairvoyant that our bodies have auras, and that there are 'objects' in these auras which can affect a person.

Since these objects can be seen, they have form - and have been described as 'thought forms'; it seems that the shape and associated colours have direct meaning, and that when similar thought forms are seen in different people, the observed effects are similar.

A brilliant thought form has usually been found to be beneficial; intrusions of dark colours (including blacks and grays) usually indicate a problem.

There are many reports that problems are so indicated in the auras of people long before a physical illness occurs; similarities in the location, shape, and colour of non-beneficial thought forms have been found to pre-date later manifestations of similar illnesses.

The ancient wisdom is that each human body has 'Chakras', shaped somewhat like microwave aerials and so acting to receive signals - from auras, our environment, and the cosmos.

We have personal patterns within our own Being that also help to define our future actions.   These may come from past lives, pre-natal impressions, childhood memories, things that we were taught, our analysis of our experiences, and our expressed dreams and hopes. These seem to be stored in our auras and our bodies.

If you send good thoughts to a person, their aura will expand. This happens even if they are thousands of miles away. What you send comes back - so avoid hurting others by having bad thoughts (anger, hate, etc) about them.

It is recognized by many that a human is sensitive to the auras of another person, and in some cases to the memories carried in these auras or in the cellular memories of a person.

Sometimes when we meet a person for the first time we move forward in our body towards him (s/he is attractive in some way), or bend backwards slightly to get away (perhaps our Being has found something undesirable).

Intuition includes the ability to receive these broadcasts and to respond to these auric interactions, processing them in the intuitive part of our thinking team, and making sense of them with the help of the logical part of our thinking team.

Hidden Energy Systems

Ancient Chinese wisdom is that there are a number of meridians running throughout a body that carry energies around a person. They have found that blockages in the meridian system are causes of ill health, and that most of these blockages occur at junction points.

Using acupuncture (inserting needles) or by acupressure (applying pressure) such blockages are removed and the movement of energies is restored - and good health returns.

It may also be that the meridian system is not confined to the physical body - that similar energy paths exist within the auras, and that there are points where these paths enter and leave the physical body.

Kirlian photography of auras has shown that energy discharges do occur at certain places - and that these points are associated with the meridian system.

This meridian system is similar to (but not the same as) the lymph system which is also carrying energies and is subject to blockages - which can be released by tapping the lymph points or 'Sore Spots'; we will be examining this as part of the EFT procedure.

The healing of these hidden energy systems may be temporary; it seems that many health problems are caused by thoughts - such as anger - leading to heart and liver problems.

Unless action is taken to release the emotions linked to such thoughts (and their associated thought forms) the ill health will return. When we hold anger, hate, or similar emotions, we hurt ourselves !

The Role of our Sub-Conscious

Very few people really understand the sub-conscious - and the models used vary between different psychologists and psychiatrists. Many of these are based on the works by Freud and Jung, but nowadays these models have been found to be deficient, and so others are being developed.

One model which is very ancient and has been proven to work over a very long time is the model used in Polynesia in general, and in Hawaii in particular by the Kahunas of Huna fame.

The Huna model has five basic levels - the God level, the Higher Self, the Conscious Self, the Sub-Conscious Self, and the physical body, operated primarily by the Sub-Conscious Self.

The God level ('The System') is all-powerful, and can do most things - but is very busy doing the most important things, so does not listen to all the 'chatter' that occurs from individuals.

The Higher Self can be considered to be our Guardian - always aware of what we are doing, but seldom interfering - except (sometimes) in an emergency.

The Conscious Self thinks that it is in control (our Ego !) and gives lots of orders, some of which are not really understood; it has a major problem in that it has great difficulty communicating directly with the Higher Self or the God level.

The Sub-Conscious Self (a label for perhaps a motley group of Beings that sometimes do not work together harmoniously !) can be considered to understand things at the level of a four or five year old child - which accounts for it not understanding some of the orders received from the Conscious Self !

But it has one great ability - it is in communication with the Higher Self. So if we request help from 'The System' we must first of all decide exactly what is wanted and express it in simple and non-contradictory terms. Next we must then persuade our Sub-Conscious that we are really sincere about getting the help - explaining clearly and precisely what is requested, and 'willing' that our Sub-Conscious ask this help from the Higher Self.

If our Higher Self is 'happy' about the request (that it will help the Human learn a lesson, or be of help to others, for example) then it will ask 'The System' to give the required assistance.

It seems as if our Sub-Conscious, Higher Self, and 'The System' are all so busy doing things that they only act if something is expressed as being done 'now'.

If it is stated in the past then it is ignored. If it is 'in the future' then they consider that no action is needed now - only in some vague and undefined future time ! So it is most important that all this asking is to happen 'NOW'.

All these models are human attempts to understand the 'inner workings' of humanity. They may not be completely correct, and some may not work well. The Huna model has been used for a great many centuries, and has a proven working history.

We are Not Alone !

Most religions preach that there is a God - or more than one; many hold that humans have 'Guardian Angels'; some accept that we have 'Spirit Guides'.

These are all labels that humans use - and the labeling may not be correct, or not be acceptable to some.

But the essence is that all have a belief that there is a power greater than humans, and that there are 'Energy Beings' who work with us in some way.

Many incidents have been reported where help was given in unusual (and sometimes miraculous) ways.

It may also be true that there are energy beings who are not helpful, that are causing problems to us - and also to the rest of creation.

So we need to find ways to get help from the 'Good Guys' and to prevent the 'bad beings' from interfering with our lives - and the lives of those dear to us.

If we try to protect ourselves by just our own efforts, there is a high probability that we will not succeed.

When we ask the help of our friends - the Good Guys - then we know that all will be well.

It seems that help is given most readily when we ask help for others; and when we express our gratitude for help given, this encourages more help to be offered !

Our Heart-Mind-Brain Team

Research has shown that the Heart has its own complement of Neurons - not as many as the Brain, but enough to be effective.

There have been a number of reports that people who have received Heart transplants become aware of memories from the donor, even to the extent of changing likes and dislikes, and altering life patterns.

It seems that your Heart is your best access to your Intuition, your link to 'The System' - which includes 'Upstairs' (non-physical influences outside of yourself), 'Downstairs' (the organs and cells within your body), as well as the level at which you normally operate, such as other people, animals, plants, and nature in general.

Little is known about the human Mind; it has not been found within the Brain, in spite of many attempts. Perhaps the Mind is outside the human body, and associated with the auras that surround humans.

The role of the Mind seems to be to operate the higher levels of the Brain - to decide the jobs that should be done, seek resources that are needed, and approve decisions prior to implementation. Perhaps the Soul or Conscious Self give leadership to the Mind.

Sometimes the Mind is by-passed, such as when an emergency occurs and the 'flight or fight' mechanism takes direct control of the Brain; research has shown that such actions originate in the lower levels of the Brain before any response can register in the higher levels.

There are various parts of the Brain, such as the reptilian and animal sections, and the more recently developed 'higher brain' found only in humans and in a few other mammals. Each part seems to have its own functions, but when damage occurs other parts have been found to take over the jobs of the damaged part.

The most important parts of the Brain (in this study) are the right and lefts parts of the higher Brain - sometimes labeled our logical and intuitive parts.

It seems that the logical part of our Brain is the home of our ego - which believes that it 'knows it all'. So one task when using our Intuition is to prevent interference by the egoistic logical Brain.

Brain Waves

Science has recognized four major ranges of Brain waves:

Name	cycles/sec	Associated Activity
Delta	0 - 4	Sleep - Deep Inner Conscious
Theta	4 - 7	Sleep - Painless Surgery - Thought - Inner Conscious
Alpha	7 - 14	Sleep - Meditation - Thought - Inner Conscious
Beta	14 - 24	Action - Outer Conscious Level - Physical Senses

There may be a fifth range, over 24 cps, about which very little is known.

It has been observed that as a human, growing from a baby to become an adult, passes through these ranges in sequence.

It seems that a person's intuitive ability becomes enhanced when in the meditative state, having Brain waves in the Alpha range - and that 10 cps, being close to the centre of that range, is a good target to select.

Understand that these Brain waves are not exclusive - different parts of a person's Brain can be operating at speeds different from other parts. A Zen Master can be operating in Theta, Alpha, and Beta at the same time, and Spiritual Healers can exceed the Zen Master by operating in Delta as well as all other speeds.

With training, most people can develop the ability to operate in Alpha and Beta at the same time, but it is best to start by getting into Alpha by itself.

A metronome can be used to signal this rate, tapes are sold which guide your Brain to so operate, and musical CD's have been developed to take you directly 'into Alpha'.

Often our Intuition is most active just as we go to sleep or awaken. This is when we pass through the 'Alpha' and other brain wave states. With practice we can 'get into' Alpha state when fully awake - and so be better able to work with our Intuition.

If you are going somewhere you usually prepare first, for example by dressing appropriately. Similarly if you want to have good Intuition then it helps to get ready - by relaxing, by being sincere, and by getting into Alpha state.

Breathing can be most helpful to you. By concentrating on your breath you tend to clear your mind, especially if you take good, deep breaths through your nose.

Dr Marcia Emery in her 'Intuition Workbook' suggests a way of using your breath to improve your intuitive abilities:

... Feel (with your consciousness, your awareness) the incoming breath at the top of your nose while drawing it down deeply into your solar plexus.

... When this area is full, expand your lungs to get more air.

... During all this time say a long 'Hang' while breathing in.

... Slowly move your consciousness down to your solar plexus, and then exhale through your mouth while saying 'Sah'.

Note that this breathing technique, especially when done slowly and with deep breathes, can help you relax and get into Alpha.

An additional help is to use your imagination while doing this exercise. With each in-breathe, imagine that plenty of life force, with healing energy, and all that is good for you, comes in and is distributed throughout your body.

When you reach the ends of your body, start a return journey, imagine collecting all the stress, tension, and problems that beset you.

As you exhale, send out all you have collected to be Healed and recycled for good.

Dr Samuel Sagan, MD, in his book 'Awakening the Third Eye', suggests that vibrating your throat just behind and below the Adam's Apple is a great benefit in speeding the transition into a meditative state.

This is similar to the way that many mystic schools teach that when calling on any Spiritual Being by name, you should vibrate that name.

He suggests that this is done by making a buzz like a bee when breathing in and out, and keeping your back straight and head upright.

If you find it difficult to make a buzz on the intake, it may be best to use the 'hang' sound, and use 'zzz' on the out breathe.

We are Energy Beings !

Physicists have shown that each atom is made of sub-atomic particles, all of which are forms of energy; and the nucleus seems to be surrounded by electrons, which are the basic form of electricity with its associated magnetism.

Such atoms combine to form molecules - and the properties of molecules differ from that of their components.

For example, hydrogen and oxygen are gases - they combine to form water which has different freezing and boiling points from the constituent elements, and can be drunk and used for cooking. When combined with other elements the properties can change to be acidic or alkaline.

The cells of our body are made from molecules - and controlled by the molecular structures that form our DNA; viruses are tiny sub-sets of DNA portions that can interfere with our own DNA in cells and cause sickness.

It seems that for animate life to exist, a form of DNA is required; conversely the DNA structure itself has a form of life - and this is so for even the sub-microscopic sized viruses.

Our body cells form all our bones, flesh, organs, nerves, neurons, and blood - our physical Being is all made of these energies doing different jobs, like teams of dancers making different dance patterns at varying speeds.

A body may have its full complement of DNA and cellular structures, but may not be alive - so there is more to life than just energy cells and electro-magnetism.

This is confirmed by the auras of people; a person whose aura is badly damaged, misshapen, extremely dark, or missing probably has little 'life force'.

Edgar Cayce was about to enter an elevator, when he noticed that he could not see any aura around any of the other people waiting to descend. He stood back, and so did not get killed with those who rode the elevator to their death when it crashed.

Cayce's record in distant Healing of people that he had never met personally also proves (to all except those who rely totally on the 'must be repeatable' proofs of non-spiritual science) that energies are involved that are not of the physical dimension, although they may operate in it.

Some people, such as Cayce, may be able to see some of these energies some of the time. Most of us do not have this ability - but we cannot see radio waves either, yet know that they exist, because we can hear their effect on a radio receiver.

Currently people know much more than those who lived a hundred years ago about the cosmos, this earth, and how electro-magnetic energies work. But we do not know it all ! And the biggest gap in our knowledge concerns other dimensions of existence.

We have a choice - we can believe that the physical dimension is the total of all creation, or we can accept that there are other dimensions.

If we choose to have an open mind, we can endeavour to improve our knowledge and understanding of such other dimensions, and find ways to work with the various energies that operate in them.

A good starting point is close to home - so let us have a closer look at ourselves and those with whom we mingle, at home, at work, and at play.

The Illusions of Stage Magicians Fool our Eyes
'All Life is an Illusion' the Heart then Cries !

We are Psychic !

Before you close this book in disgust, are you sure that you understand what is meant by 'Psychic' ?

'Psychic' means 'belonging to, or associated with, the Psyche'.

Looking in Webster's dictionary, Psyche is a Greek word meaning Soul or Mind.

So if you are not Psychic, does this mean that you lack a Soul or are Mindless ?

Since we know that we are a Soul (or some sort of 'other dimensional' Energy Being) that is having an experience in a Human Being in the physical dimension, perhaps our Soul has some sensing abilities that differ from those of the physical human body.

If the Soul is associated with the Human Being, then perhaps some senses belonging to the Soul are used - even without the Human Being's awareness of such use.

The Human Being may be so accustomed to these senses being used that they do not realize that the senses are those of the Soul, and not those of a 'normal' Human Being.

Successful Teachers

People who are recognized as being successful in teaching or in persuading others to accept their point of view are those who know that some people have a strong sense of 'seeing' (It looks good), of 'feeling' (It feels good), of 'hearing' (Sounds good to me), or of just 'knowing' (I know it is good).

So to get their message to reach all their students they express their teachings in different ways - so that every person that listens has the message told in ways that appeal to them.

Notice that the human senses of tasting, smelling, and of balancing are not used.

Let us examine the way that such people operate.

Feelers

People who have a strong sense of feeling often get that feeling in the area known as the 'Solar Plexus' - hence the popular expression of 'having a gut feeling about ...'.

People naturally turn their body to face objects or people when they want to sense them more deeply; when people feel uncomfortable they often cross your arms in front of their solar plexus area to feel more protected and less vulnerable.

If a Feeler walks into a room where there has been an argument or some other severe discord, the Feeler instantly knows that the 'atmosphere' in the room is 'bad' - and perhaps may get a hint as to the cause.

They will get a 'Danger Ahead' feeling if there are problems with being in a place or with a person that can lead to trouble; they are aware of the 'not good' subtle energies.

Feelers are sensitive to the feelings of others, both good and bad, so they find it hard to remain detached from others. They are 'people people' who give of themselves, and adapt themselves to keep others happy.

They are usually living in the 'now', and so not be too concerned with time; deadlines can wait !

When with a person who is angry about something, a Feeler will know that the anger is there, and often assume incorrectly that the anger is directed at the Feeler.

If a Feeler is in close contact with a person that is sick, the Feeler may often feel the pain - and assume that it is him/her self that is becoming ill.

The biggest problem is learning to understand that many of the feelings that they have are those of others, not their own. Failing this lesson, they can become emotionally overwhelmed.

Hearers

One of the main indications that you are a 'Hearer' is 'talking with yourself' - actually you may be discussing things with thinking life forms that are within your own mind; this is especially so when you hear a response that you did not originate.

Often these thoughts, words, or phrases seem to come from the centre of you head, as an 'inner sound'. A song may keep playing in your mind - perhaps it is hinting at a solution to a problem, or guiding you to take a particular action, either based on the words of the song or circumstances when you previously listened to the song.

When listening to others, the Hearer may hear things 'between the lines' - perhaps hearing the truth that the person who is speaking is trying to hide.

If a Hearer has not decided an issue, the Hearer will ask questions continually until they have a full understanding. Straight forward answers are best, since the Hearer will take them as being exact; subtleties are seldom understood.

Once a situation is clear in their mind, the decision will be told assertively, with most of the detail needed for implementation - to a Hearer the use of tact and diplomacy only tend to confuse communication !

Hearers can be over-analytical, ask too many questions, often come on too strong, and may radiate too much mental energy.

If you say you will do something, a Hearer expects it do be done correctly - and on time; just 'doing your best' is not enough.

See-ers - or Seers for short !

Men and women who are strong in seeing tend to live their life from a visual perspective. Such a person experiences life as one vivid mental image after another.

Whether planning a meal or one's life work, the ability to see the entire picture is his or her most important reference point and greatest strength.

Seers must have an inner picture; without it they feel lost; they like to have light - and they want it everywhere, sometimes to the consternation of others ! They frequently leave lights on when they leave a room because they want them to be on already when they come back.

A distinctive characteristic of Seers is their initial resistance to change. They have an internal picture of how they expect everything to be, which is their security and reference point.

When someone wants to change that picture, or presents a new idea (no matter how good) that complicates the plan, they will resist strongly. Their whole Being will scream, *"Don't change my picture!"*

This can make Seers seem rigid and inflexible; if you force an immediate answer about a picture change, you will always get a resounding *"No !"*

The secret of success is to introduce the idea calmly and give the person time to reshape his or her inner image. When an idea is introduced without pressure, Seers eventually visualize a way to work the change into the total plan, because they are well able to see problems, can visualize solutions, and are good at seeing fine detail.

If you are a Seer, sleeping on ideas is an excellent policy. Allow yourself time to reshape your perspective. So don't say *"No !"* immediately, but *"Let me think about that and get back to you tomorrow."* Allow yourself to day-dream - you will usually come up with an even better master plan that incorporates the new idea.

Seers like to have a good view, to see other people at a dining table; they are good at packing items and arranging things; they have good colour co-ordination, and an excellent sense of direction.

They can be rigid and inflexible because they do not want their picture changed - and often will not act until they have the whole picture. They are worriers, visualizing all that could go wrong, and so can tend toward perfectionism (wanting a perfect picture); they may be very self-critical (seeing and emphasizing their faults more than strengths).

Knowers - aka Gnostics

Some people just 'know' the answer to a problem, what is going to happen, or what to do at any time. This knowledge may come extremely fast; the impression received may be fleeting, without any substance, reasoning, or supporting information - and so be hard to understand or even accept.

The instant information that a Gnostic receives enables excellent anticipation of problems or difficulties, helps to adjust rapidly to changing circumstances and make better decisions, and be at the right place at the right time. Knowers do not waste time worrying needlessly ! But they sometimes are easily bored, and frequently don't complete a project.

Because this 'knowing' is so fleeting, so spontaneous, sometimes a Gnostic may not have the full perspective so necessary for mature judgment.

This instant knowing can be a great help in relationships with other people. As a Knower you may be surprised at how these insights can improve your understanding of (and communication with) other people - especially those with whom you have business or personal problems; and how instinctively you know the needs of family members and loved ones.

The insightfulness of the Knower can provide information and answers that are otherwise unavailable; it is an unlimited open channel to the universe that can tap a wealth of creative methods and approaches - often not restricted by convention

Gnostics can be scattered by the volume of thoughts and ideas they receive, and may pick up information far in advance - and sometimes too soon, with the result that they are often ahead of other people's timing and are resented for it.

They can speak too quickly, blurting out what comes to mind without thinking it over first.

Interactions

The most complex challenges that face most of us each and every day are our relationships with other people - at home, at work, and at play.   Each individual is unique - and sometimes difficult to understand.

How you deal with others is often the key to success - or the cause of failure. Recognizing these differences in sensing can help by giving you new and more creative insights to apply to interpersonal relationships.

Seers must have their inner picture to feel solid, without their pictures they are like Knowers stripped of their knowingness or Feelers forced to stay in a discomforting environment.

While a Seer needs not only to see the total picture but to see it with all its connections, the Hearer is more concerned with understanding how the current situation can be explained. Just as the Hearer wants to understand why, the Seer want to see how things fit together.

Without that complete view the Seer is as unmovable as the Hearer is without his understanding.

In contrast, the Feeler and the Knower do not require an inner picture plan. Feelers are wishing to 'go with the flow' - as long as things feel comfortable they will enjoy the moment without much concern for the future. Knowers know that the plan will come to them in time, so they continue to rely on their instincts to adapt from moment to moment.

There is a logical progression from knowing to hearing. People tend to confuse the two at times because both have an inner mental quality. Hearing can serve as a sort of inner computer, a way to analyze the insights of knowingness.

Your Own Abilities

Now that you are aware of the various Soul-Mind senses, you may have decided which senses are strong for yourself; usually a person will be strong in one sense, and have another sense almost as strong.

Some people have been gifted with a very strong sense, which may even be as strong as their physical senses - such as those people who are naturally clairvoyant.

According to reports some clairvoyants have been surprised to find that other people cannot see the things that they see naturally.

Most people are not so gifted - but can improve their own abilities; the best way to start is to first improve the senses that you know are your own strongest.

Improve your Feeling

Pay special attention to the different feelings that you get when you meet others and go in various places. Especially learn to recognize that many of these feelings are NOT YOUR OWN !

When you feel anger, hate, or even pain on meeting another person, know that you are using your feeling sense to link with them - it is fine to help understand their problems, but do not take them on as your own !

If you get a sudden pain in your stomach, assume that you are linking to the pain in the other person. You may be an empath !

Be aware of the different feelings that you have when you go to a happy celebration such as a wedding, or a sad time such as a funeral.

Cast your mind back to such situations - you will be surprised to find that you can recall your feelings of the vibrations very easily.

Similarly compare the feelings that you get in a crowded shop or market with those that you recall from relaxing on the beach or in a beautiful spot.

The more that you practice your awareness of the different feelings that you get in various places and situations, the better able you will become in recognizing the energy patterns that give you such feelings in other places and situations.

Louder Soul Hearing

If you are aware that you talk to yourself, understand that you are not going mad ! Usually the talk that you hear is very quiet, and seems to be right in the middle of your head.

You may even hear a background noise most of the time; your Heart-Mind-Brain system is like a radio, hearing all transmissions but amplifying only the signal that is chosen by tuning.

But your Soul may be interested in signals that are not just for you as a Human Being; for example, it may be tuning into another person to see if they need assistance or perhaps have intent that would be detrimental to you.

The key with hearing is to listen to the thoughts that come to you, especially those that you did not consciously originate.

As you progress you may find that you can ask your Heart a question and hear the answer ! But be aware that your ego may also be feeding you thoughts - so it pays to check with your Heart whether the thought came from your Intuition or your ego.

People with a strong sense of hearing may have problems when meditating - hearing a constant stream of 'chatter'. It may help to speak to your Heart and ask it to reduce (or to eliminate) all thoughts that are from sources other than your Heart.

How to See More

The better your visualization, the more that you can see; see an apple, cut it and visualize the outside and inside. Now imagine that the colours change - a blue skin and green inside, with yellow pips, and perhaps a red maggot.

Look at the apple from different directions, change the colours, and then 'morph' it into a tomato or cabbage, visualizing all the details.

Visualize your home, and other homes in which you have lived or visited; peer into cupboards, look in the refrigerator, admire the garden.

The most interesting fact is that your Heart-Mind-Brain team is lazy; so rather than go to the great effort of making a pretend picture, it is easier, more fun, and less effort to use the ability of the Soul to visit and then show what is actually there !

Do not expect to get a beautifully coloured picture in full detail. That may happen in dream state, or when you become extremely efficient - but you can expect to just 'know' the overall picture, or somehow have an understanding of what is there.

Your 'Mind's Eye' does not normally use the same procedures as your physical sight, and is usually located in your forehead. If you are looking straight ahead, note where you feel that your eyes are pointing, and then close your eyes - now probably you will feel your sight to be directed via a point in your forehead.

Knowing Even More

Pay attention to your hunches ! They come and go very fast, and may not be complete in detail. But you can always ask your Heart for more information.

The best way is to formulate a YES/NO question in your logical mind, stand, and ask your Heart - as you did in the very first exercise.

Remember it is the very first idea that 'pops' into your mind that counts - further replies may be ego saying 'nonsense' !

You can play games like 'Twenty Questions' or 'Animal, Vegetable, Mineral ?' to extend your understanding of the hunch.

Practice makes Perfect

If you do not succeed at first, have another go. If you do not keep on making the effort, how can you succeed ?

Remember that all the great players (of music, sports, etc) practice - and then practice more !

You may not become perfect in every way, but you will definitely improve your skill and ability - so it is very worthwhile.

Your attitude is critical; believe that you will succeed - and that you deserve to succeed. If you have any doubts, or believe that it is wrong for some reason, then you are sabotaging yourself.

In all these cases, allow your imagination to roam free. Do not force things, just allow things to happen. Be gentle in all your thoughts and actions, and show appreciation and gratitude for every gain that you make - your 'Being-ness' and 'Upstairs' like to be thanked, and when given gratitude will make more effort to help you !

Having even the slightest success is proof that you have the ability, and can improve your skill. Such experience is far more powerful than anything you are told or read in books. Have faith in yourself !

More Information

Much of the above has been summarized from the book 'You Are Psychic !' written by Pete A. Sanders Jr., published by Fawcett Columbine, ISBN 0-449-90507-1; it is the best book that I have read to explain the interaction of Soul and Body senses - and how to work with them to increase your abilities to use these senses.

The book describes the Soul Energy Being to be located above a persons head, with a link down to the brain's control centre (the pituary / pineal glands); a person's 'awareness' (the ability to feel the location of a pain, for example) may be moving (or extending) this link to locations within the body - and, with practice, to places outside the body.

Pete describes the Soul Senses as being guided by funnels. He visualizes a funnel located between the solar plexus and diaphragm as the main input for feelings - which is why so many people place their arms to cover this place when with others.

The other funnels are aimed at the area of the pituary / pineal glands; the Soul Seeing funnel is in the area around the centre of the forehead, the Soul Hearing funnels (one each side) are above the ears, and the Soul Knowing funnel goes upward from the top of the head.

The book gives exercises to recognize these senses and to improve your skills in using them.

Pete Sanders is the leading light in the 'Free Soul' organization, which organizes home-study and instructor-led courses. The web site is **www.freesoul.net** *and their postal address Box 1762, Sedona, Arizona 86339. You can also telephone him at (928)282-9425.*

We Compute !

Another way of visualizing a Human Being is as a bio-computer - a self-contained personal computer that can link to a higher level main-frame computer or to the universal/cosmic internet, using modem-like wireless connections. Our Heart is like the CPU (Central Processing Unit).

There are many similarities to an electro-magnetic computer - we have an operating system (our belief system), short term working memory in our mind, medium term memory in our brain, long term memory in our body cells, and mystics tell of memory like a tape backup held in the Akashic records.

When we listen and speak we work at a slow speed - similar to the way that typing on a keyboard is far slower than the speed at which our computer handles data. Even when just thinking, our speed of operation is much slower than when we relax completely - such as when having a snooze.

I have found that if I study the data in the morning, and have a quick snooze at lunchtime, then when I awaken I know the way to process the data efficiently and successfully - this has been a great help in my career as a Chartered Engineer and as a Professional Engineer.

Our sub-conscious keeps things running in the background - even when our input devices (eyes, ears, etc) are switched off when we sleep.

It does this because it is running programs - installed by the manufacturer, loaded in our operating system, told by others (perhaps virus infected), or formed as the result of our experiences.

We run programs all the time - the most powerful being those in our operating system, based on the beliefs that we hold.

Luckily we can change programs, getting rid of those not now wanted and adding new ones - although we may sometimes need expert assistance to install upgrades to the operating system.

Religions could be likened to proprietary operating systems, having minor variations depending on the cultural and national environments.

Some may be better than others for various purposes, but often they are not compatible with other systems.

Perhaps the best operating systems are those that are open, not controlled by any one company, or not adjusted for only one environment - similar to having an open mind.

Opening Our Operating System

The best way to have an open mind is to not have any firm beliefs; to categorize all that we have been told, even all our experiences, as being like pieces of a jig-saw puzzle that we are trying to solve.

When we look at a piece, we can see various attributes according to the way that it is seen, the direction our gaze holds, and the effects of different lighting - and what we expect to see !

We may have been told that certain pieces MUST fit together in a particular place; those who gave us these hints helped as best they could, but perhaps did not have an identical puzzle, or understand the complete picture.

We try to fit all the pieces together, but often come across a new piece that can only go in the middle of some collection (a program, perhaps) that has been assembled - so we have to take those pieces apart and re-arrange them to make a better fit.

If we refused to make such re-arrangements we could never improve the picture - the puzzle would never be solved.

The more that we do assemble the overall picture, the more likely that we will find pieces that do not fit at all in our own puzzle - they belong to other puzzles owned by other people, and have got mixed up with our pieces.

Running Programs

There are many different parts to our brain - most well known are our reptilian brain, our animal brain, and our advanced brain with its logical and intuitive halves. These all work together, like the different components in a computer.

It seems that when any new information is received, it is checked by the reptilian brain to see if it corresponds to any previous action, and if any 'fight or flight' action is needed - which takes precedence over all other action.

This has been found to occur before any knowledge is passed to the 'thinking' part of our Mind-Brain system.

Failing 'fight or flight' action, but finding correspondence with a previous situation recorded in our memory banks, the actions then taken may be prepared for re-use.

This is especially so if there is any emotion attached to the memory; then an 'emotional trigger' may be operated - which sets in motion a repeat of the previous actions, even if these are not the best actions to take.

We will examine ways that we can overcome these 'emotional triggers' in later chapters.

Adding and Changing Programs

When we started to ride a bicycle it was hard work, falling off a number of times, because we had not learnt the skill of balancing on a bike.

As we progressed, the skill became an ability that was now natural to us; the program had been installed, so that whenever we got on a bike we ran the 'bike riding program'.

All our life we have added programs in this way - starting to crawl and then walk; learning to talk, read, and write; finding how our behavior was accepted.

As we expanded our contacts, we may have realized that sometimes our behavior had to be modified to work with others and so get what we wanted - and we changed our programs.

Sometimes making a change is difficult - we know what we want to achieve, but perhaps our operating system creates obstacles or sub-programs that are unknowingly involved, and also need to be revised.

To succeed, our conscious mind has to be clear and precise about what is needed - not how it will happen.

This must then be explained in simple language, remembering that most of our sub-conscious mind operates at the level of a four or five year old child - so keep it simple !

Our sub-conscious mind understands pictures better than words, so visualizing the desired effect is important - and emphasizing this by emotions, feelings, and other senses is a great help, since our sub-conscious mind is closely linked to our senses.

Our sub-conscious mind is not well able to differentiate between what we imagine and what is an actual happening in the physical world - especially so if our imagination includes the operation of our various senses. This is most useful in persuading our sub-conscious to make a change.

It is also important to do all this 'in the NOW' - if it is past, then it is so; if in the future, then it is not to be done now. Remember that the sub-conscious mind is not logical - it may have its own logic, but it is very different from that of our logical mind, the way that we think with our normal consciousness.

Affirmations

When we have decided the required end result, we can use our logical mind to define an affirmation that represents this result in a clear and precise way, using simple language.

The sub-conscious does not understand NOT; it considers this word to be similar to NOW, and so any affirmation which includes NOT is taken to be confirming the opposite intent !

Ways to overcome this included to affirm that you are 'free from' [the unwanted], and that you are [the opposite].

The best time to make affirmations is when we are in that state between being awake and sleeping - as we go to sleep, and as we awake, including any times when we awake temporarily during our sleep period.

It is helpful to repeat any affirmation three times; the first time is an incidence, the second time may be a co-incidence, but the third time indicates that it is really meant !

One problem that has been identified is the verbal structure. Many times a child may have been told something in the third person such as *"You are stupid !"* - and coming as a judgment from others it is taken to be fact.

To overcome this, it helps to couch any correction in ways that include the third person *"you ... "*, then the impersonal third person, and finally the first person *"I ... "*.

Let us consider an example; you have been told:

> *"You are stupid (or inadequate in some aspect)".*

The basic affirmation could be:

> *"I am intelligent (more than adequate in that aspect) !"*

This may best be expressed (three times as shown):

> *"In each and every moment of each and every day,*
> *You, [your name], are intelligent in every way"*
> *"In each and every moment of each and every day,*
> *You, [your name], are intelligent in every way"*
> *"In each and every moment of each and every day,*
> *You, [your name], are intelligent in every way"*

Then three times more, this time impersonally:

> *"In each and every moment of each and every day,*
> *[your name] is intelligent in every way"*

And finally, three times in the first person:

> *"In each and every moment of each and every day,*
> *I, [your name], am intelligent in every way"*

This may seem tedious, but if you really want the change to occur it may be well worth-while; remember to put lots of feeling and emotion into these statements, and do your best to imagine with all your senses that the results are now existing - they have been achieved already.

How often should this sequence be repeated ?

Opinions vary, but it is probably correct to say for at least three days; if the effect is not manifested, keep on until it does happen.

Do not make any affirmation too long - each affirmation should cover one single aspect, not a whole string of things to be changed.

If there are many aspects to be changed, then do this using separate affirmations.

Direct Programming

Another way to implement a new or changed program is to write down its details, then ask your Heart if this is correctly understood. If not, revise it until it is understood.

Ask your Heart if this program is in your highest and best interest - if not, then do not proceed, but you can ask your Heart to hint why this is so, and perhaps write a variation that is beneficial.

Otherwise ask your Heart if any changes would improve the program; the very first hint that comes to mind is probably from your Intuition - incorporate this into your program, and ask again.

Repeat this until you do not get any more hints. Then ask your Heart to install and implement the program, and afterwards ask if the installation was successful and will be fully implemented in all cases - if not, ask why.

It takes less time, but more concentrated effort, to install a program this way, but the detailing can be more extensive - you are working with your Heart, not just your sub-conscious.

Another advantage of using this method is that it can build a number of sub-programs which can be re-used in other programs; these can be called in exactly the same way that one computer program can call and link with another.

Programming Example

Perhaps the most important program to load is one that permits direct programming itself - to check that your Heart is willing and able to do the work expected.

First install a sub-program:

"That my Heart be in command of my total Being at all times, in all ways, and in all aspects" - so do this as explained above; if any problem is encountered, install this as an affirmation.

Now the main program:

"That my Heart will assist and co-operate with all in my total Being to ensure the correct and satisfactory installation and implementation of all affirmations and programs which I ask to be installed, providing that all changes made are for my highest and best good, shall not cause harm to others, and shall be in effect until revised or cancelled by me".

This is another program that is most beneficial:

"That all calls that I make to my Intuition shall be via my Heart, and that all replies that are given shall be the truth as best I am able to understand, based on information obtained from all possible sources, provided that if the information is not available or the reply should not be given then this will be so indicated".

Never, ever, try to impose any affirmation or program on any person except yourself!

Debugging Programs

Any ideas why this is so called ?

In the early days of computers, when instructions were issued by punched cards (which, incidentally, were based on weaving technology !) sometimes a bug would get caught in one of the punched holes - and so change the program.

This has been extended to identifying problems in computers (bugs like warm places) as well as in programs; many of the programs now used (and the computers themselves) are far more complicated than in the old days - as, perhaps, are humans.

Luckily there are some debugging programs available to those 'in the know'.

One of the best for use in 'human computers' is the 'Emotional Freedom Techniques' program developed by Gary Craig - we will have a 'first look' at this in the next chapter.

Improving Access to Storage

The conscious mind tends to operate on information in a linear fashion, such as reasoning that A+B=C.

The sub-conscious mind, however, deals with this as ABC - and it finds the answer to a question based on whether any of these, A, B, or C, are held in a particular storage space.

To take material from short term memory and store it for future use, use the following procedure:

1. Focus your awareness, your attention, between your eyes on the thought or concept that you want to store - you will feel this as energy or pressure in the upper frontal lobes of your brain.

2. Wrap your awareness around the energy, holding the concept very clearly and firmly in your mind until you know it thoroughly; you do not have to think about every detail, just hold the entire concept in your consciousness as one total 'lump' - like holding a mass of cotton-wool balls, without worrying about any individual ball.

3. Now pull the energy downwards towards the base of your head at the rear, and imagine a trap-door opening.

This opens the 'reticular formation', and allows the energy of the information to flow down into the cells of the body, to be stored in a holographic way.

4. Keep pulling the energy into your body, until you feel it harmonize and settle into the energy systems of your body.

You can access stored information very simply:

1. Place your awareness on a subject and ask that it be retrieved from memory.

2. Relax - do not put any energy or stress on the subject ! Just 'Space Off' - without thinking intently about anything else.

3. The information will 'appear' in your Mind-Brain system, ready for you to use.

This method, especially the retrieval method, can help you get good marks in an examination !

Like most skills, the more that you use this technique, the easier that it becomes - and the greater your confidence in knowing that you will get information when you need it.

With extended use you may find that just one bit of information can trigger entirely new ways of understanding the information - and lead to new concepts of thought.

Where Astonishing Emotional Relief
Leads to Profound Physical Healings

Emotional Freedom Techniques

Applies to all issues, including....

Pain Relief	Fears & Phobias	Relationship Issues
Anger	Blood Pressure	Respiratory Problems
Addictions	Weight Loss	Children's Issues
Anxiety	Trauma	Women's Issues
Depression	School, Sports, & Sexual Performance Issues	
Allergies	Serious Diseases (from migraines to cancer)	

"Some day the medical profession will wake up and realize that unresolved emotional issues are the main cause of 85% of all illnesses. When they do, EFT will be one of their primary healing tools .... as it is for me."

Eric Robins, MD

Gary Craig, the Founder and Developer of EFT, writes about the free manual - which can be downloaded from **www.emofree.com**

"This manual is a starting point - an introduction - to EFT. It is a companion to our more extensive video based EFT Course and is NOT intended to be complete training.

Study this manual and diligently apply the concepts herein to yourself and you will likely get immediate, and often profound, results.

This is the promise of EFT and one you should realize quite easily upon proper application. You will also find occasions where you stub your toe and will scratch your head while asking: "Why doesn't it work in this case ?" or "Why does it work on everyone else but not me ?" or "Why does it seem to be permanent in some cases and only temporary in others ?", etc.

These questions are all answerable but the answers are not found in a manual such as this. They come from experience and more detailed training.

That's why diligent students should go beyond this manual and get our affordable DVDs at https://www.emofree.com/store/store.aspx.

An aspiring surgeon can only learn so much from a book but, after that, s/he needs to observe the process in action by those who have mastered it. There is an art to delivering EFT that is profusely illustrated in our DVDs. Those who wish to develop this art will need this additional training.

EFT was originally designed to overhaul the psychotherapy profession. Fortunately, that goal has been reached as EFT has dramatically reduced therapy time from months or years down to minutes or hours.

Along the way, we kept noticing that profound physical healings were also taking place. Vision improved, headaches disappeared, cancer pains and symptoms subsided and so on. The reason for this, we found, is that EFT addresses causes that Western Healing Practices have largely ignored.

Medicine, for example, pays very little attention to disruptions in the body's energy meridians nor does it give much weight to emotional causes. These causes, of course, are the centerpieces of EFT.

Thus it is no wonder that EFT produces benefits where the medical profession has thrown up its hands.

The reason is simply because we are taking aim at causes that others have largely disregarded.

This EFT Manual was written before I realized the profound and widespread nature of the physical healings. Accordingly, it stresses the emotional healings and doesn't cover the physical healings in nearly as dramatic a fashion as they actually occur.

Because it has proven to be such an effective teaching manual, however, I have decided to leave it as is rather than modify it to emphasize physical healings.

It is the emotional and energetic causes that we need to understand and those are profusely illustrated in these pages."

An Even More Brief Introduction to EFT

This has been extracted from Gary's manual, with his kind permission, to give you an idea of what EFT involves - and how you can immediately get experience in helping yourself.

The Basic Recipe

Like baking a cake, each ingredient must be performed precisely as described, and they must be introduced in the proper order. Otherwise - no result

The Basic Recipe is very simple and easy to do. Once memorized, each round of it can be performed in about 1 minute. It will take some practice, of course, but after a few tries the whole process becomes familiar and you can bake that emotional freedom cake in your sleep.

You will then be well on your way to mastery of EFT and all the rewards it provides. Various shortcuts are available and described in the manual and in the videos.

The Basic Recipe consists of four ingredients, two of which are identical. They are:

1. The Setup
2. The Sequence
3. The 9 Gamut Procedure
4. The Sequence

The Setup

This routine is vital to the whole process and prepares the energy system so that the rest of the Basic Recipe can do its job.

Your energy system is like a set of subtle electric circuits. It can be subject to a form of interference which can block the balancing effect of these tapping procedures.

When present, this interfering blockage must be removed or the Basic Recipe will not work - this removal is the job of The Setup.

Technically speaking, this interfering blockage takes the form of a polarity reversal within your energy system. This is not the same thing as the energy disruptions which cause your negative emotions; it is similar to putting the negative and positive terminals of a battery the wrong way round in a radio or other device - not that you stop working, but some parts do not work properly.

This polarity reversal has an official name. It is called 'Psychological Reversal' and represents a fascinating discovery with wide ranging applications to all areas of healing, and to personal performance.

It is the reason why some diseases are chronic and respond very poorly to conventional treatments. It is also the reason why some people have such a difficult time losing weight or giving up an addictive substance.

It is, quite literally, the cause of self sabotage. An entire course could be dedicated to its uses ! For now, however, we need only know some foundational things about Psychological Reversal that apply to EFT - and more importantly, how to correct it.

Psychological Reversal is caused by self defeating, negative thinking which often occurs subconsciously and thus outside of your awareness.

On average, it will be present (and thus hinder EFT) about 40% of the time. Some people have very little of it (this is rare) while others are beset by it most of the time (this also is rare). Most people fall somewhere in between these two extremes.

It doesn't create any feelings within you, so you won't know if it is present or not.

When it is present it will stop any attempt at healing, including EFT, dead in its tracks. Therefore, it must be corrected if the rest of the Basic Recipe is going to work.

It only takes 8 or 10 seconds to do and, if it isn't present, no harm is done. If it is present, however, a major impediment to your success will be out of the way.

There are two parts to the Setup:

1. You repeat an affirmation 3 times while you...
2. Rub the 'Sore Spot' or, alternatively, tap the 'Karate Chop Point' (these will be explained shortly).

The Affirmation

Since the cause of Psychological Reversal involves negative thinking it should come as no surprise that the correction for it includes a neutralizing affirmation. Such is the case and here it is:

> *"Even though I have this* _____
> *I deeply and completely accept myself."*

The blank is filled with a brief description of the problem you want to address. Here are some examples:

> *"Even though I have this fear of public speaking,*
>   *I deeply and completely accept myself"*
> *"Even though I have this headache, I deeply . . ."*
> *"Even though I have this anger towards my father, I deeply . . ."*
> *"Even though I have this war memory, I deeply . . ."*
> *"Even though I have this stiffness in my neck, I deeply . . ."*
> *"Even though I have these nightmares, I deeply . . ."*
> *"Even though I have this craving for alcohol, I deeply . . ."*
> *"Even though I have this fear of snakes, I deeply . . ."*
> *"Even though I have this depression,*
>   *I deeply and completely accept myself"*

This is only a partial list, of course, because the possible issues that are addressable by EFT are endless.

You use affirmations like...

"I accept myself even though I have this . . ."
"Even though I have this . . .,
  I deeply and profoundly accept myself"
"I love and accept myself even though I have this . . "

All of these affirmations are correct because they follow the same general format - they acknowledge the problem and create self acceptance despite the existence of the problem.

That is what is necessary for the affirmation to be effective.

You can use any of them but the recommended one is excellent - it is easily memorizable and has a good track record of doing the job.

Now here are some interesting points about the affirmation:

... It doesn't matter whether you believe the affirmation or not - just say it.

... It is better to say it with feeling and emphasis, but saying it routinely will usually do the job.

... It is best to say it out loud, but if you are in a social situation where you prefer to mutter it under your breath, or do silently - then go ahead. It will probably be effective.

To add to the effectiveness of the affirmation, the Setup also includes the simultaneous rubbing of a 'Sore Spot' or tapping on the 'Karate Chop Point'. They are described next.

The Sore Spot

There are two Sore Spots and it doesn't matter which one you use. They are located in the upper left and right portions of the chest and you find them as follows:

Go to the base of the throat about where a man would knot his tie. Poke around in this area and you will find a U shaped notch at the top of your sternum (breastbone).

From the top of that notch go down 3 inches toward your navel and then sideways 3 inches to your left (or right). You should now be in the upper left (or right) portion of your chest. If you press vigorously in that area (within a 2 inch radius) you will find a 'Sore Spot'. This is the place you will need to rub while saying the affirmation.

This spot is sore when you rub it vigorously because lymphatic congestion occurs there. When you rub it, you are dispersing that congestion. Fortunately, after a few episodes the congestion is all dispersed and the soreness goes away. Then you can rub it with no discomfort whatsoever.

You are unlikely to have massive, intense pain by rubbing this Sore Spot. It is certainly bearable and should not cause any undue discomfort.

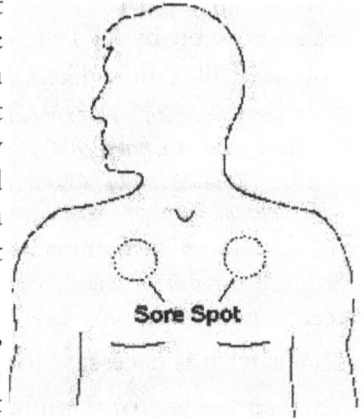

Sore Spot

If it does hurt, then lighten up your pressure a little.

Also, if you've had some kind of operation in that area of the chest (or if there's any medical reason whatsoever why you shouldn't be probing around in that specific area) then switch to the other side. Both sides are equally effective.

In any case, if there is any doubt, consult your health practitioner before proceeding, or tap the 'Karate Chop Point' instead.

The Karate Chop Point - KC

The Karate Chop Point (abbreviated KC) is located at the center of the fleshy part of the outside of either hand between the top of the wrist and the base of the baby finger - the part of your hand you would use to deliver a karate chop.

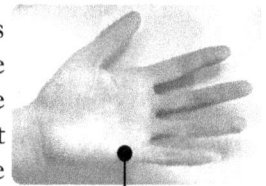

KC

Instead of rubbing it as you would the Sore Spot, you vigorously tap the Karate Chop Point with the fingertips of the index finger and middle finger of the other hand.

While you could use the Karate Chop Point of either hand, it is usually most convenient to tap the Karate Chop Point of the non-dominant hand with the two fingertips of the dominant hand.

If you are right handed, for example, you would tap the Karate Chop Point on the left hand with the fingertips of the right hand.

Should you use the Sore Spot or the Karate Chop Point ?

After years of experience with both of these methods, it has been determined that rubbing the Sore Spot is more effective than tapping the Karate Chop Point.

It doesn't have a commanding lead by any means - but it is preferred.

Because The Setup is so important in clearing the way for the rest of the Basic Recipe to work, I urge you to use the Sore Spot rather than the Karate Chop Point. It puts the odds a little more in your favor.

However, the Karate Chop Point is perfectly useful and will clear out any interfering blockage in the vast majority of cases.

So feel free to use it if the Sore Spot is inappropriate for any reason.

Stepping Through It

Now that you understand the parts to The Setup, performing it is easy. You create a word or short phrase to fill in the blank in the affirmation and then simply repeat the affirmation 3 times while continuously rubbing the Sore Spot or tapping the Karate Chop Point. Do this with emphasis for best results.

That's it. After a few practice rounds, you should be able to perform The Setup in 8 seconds or so.

Now, with The Setup properly performed, you are ready for the next ingredient in the Basic Recipe - The Sequence.

The Sequence

The Sequence is very simple in concept. It involves tapping on the end points of the major energy meridians in the body and is the method by which the energy system is balanced out.

You can tap with either hand but it is usually more convenient to do so with your dominant hand (right hand if you are right handed).

Tap with the fingertips of your index finger and middle finger. This covers a little larger area than just tapping with one fingertip and allows you to cover the tapping points more easily.

Tap solidly but never so hard as to hurt or bruise yourself.

Tap about 7 (5 to 9, for example) times on each of the tapping points. About 7 times is needed because you will be repeating a 'reminder phrase' (covered later) while tapping and it will be difficult to count at the same time.

Most of the tapping points exist on either side of the body. It doesn't matter which side you use nor does it matter if you switch sides during The Sequence. For example, you can tap under your right eye and, later in The Sequence, tap under your left arm.

The Points

Each energy meridian has two end points. For the purposes of The Basic Recipe, you need only tap on one end to balance out any disruptions that may exist in it.

These end points are near the surface of the body and are thus more readily accessed than other points along the meridians that may be more deeply buried.

What follows are instructions on how to locate the end points of those meridians that are important to The Basic Recipe. Taken together, and done in the order presented, they form The Sequence.

1. Eye Brow - EB

At the beginning of the eyebrow, just above and to one side of the nose.

2. Side of the Eye - SE

On the bone bordering the outside corner of the eye.

3. Under the Eye - UE

On the bone under an eye about 1 inch below your pupil.

4. Under the Nose - UN

On the small area between the bottom of your nose and the top of your upper lip.

5. Chin - Ch

Midway between the point of your chin and the bottom of your lower lip. Even though it is not directly on the point of the chin, we call it the chin point because it is descriptive enough.

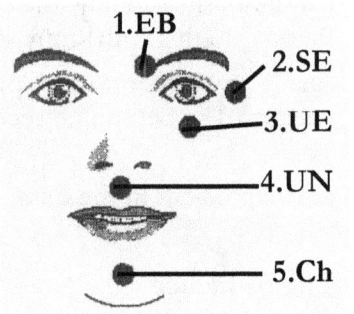

6. Collar Bone - CB

The junction where the sternum (breastbone), collarbone and the first rib meet. To locate it, first place your forefinger on the U-shaped notch at the top of the breastbone (about where a man would knot his tie), then from the bottom of the U, move your forefinger down toward the navel 1 inch and then go to the left (or right) 1 inch towards the side of the body.

7. Under the Arm - UA

At a point even with the nipple (for men) or in the middle of the bra strap (for women). It is about 4 inches below the armpit.

6.CB

Sore Spot

8. Below Nipple - BN

7.UA

For men, one inch below the nipple. For ladies, where the underskin of the breast meets the chest wall.

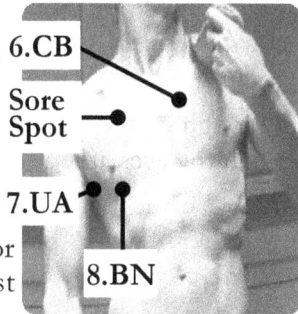

8.BN

9. Thumb -Th

On the outside edge of your thumb at a point even with the base of the thumbnail.

10. Index Finger - IF

Inside Fingers

On the side of your index finger (the side facing your thumb) at a point even with the base of the fingernail.

11. Middle Finger - MF

On the side of your middle finger (the side closest to your thumb) at a point even with the base of the fingernail.

**9.Th (not shown)
10.IF, 11.MF,
12.BF shown.**

12. Baby Finger. - BF

On the inside of your baby finger (the side closest to your thumb) at a point even with the base of the fingernail.

13. Karate Chop Point - KC

This has been described under the section on The Setup.

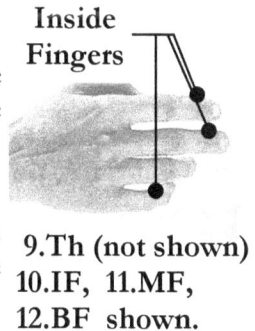

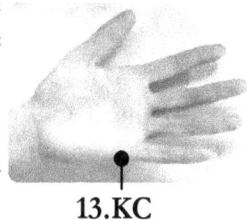

13.KC

Order of Tapping

Note that these tapping points proceed down the body - each tapping point is below the one before it. That should make the order of tapping a snap to memorize.

The 9 Gamut Procedure

The purpose of the 9 Gamut Procedure is to 'fine tune' the brain and it does so via some eye movements and some humming and counting.

Through connecting nerves, certain parts of the brain are stimulated when the eyes are moved.

Likewise the right side of the brain (the creative side) is engaged when you hum a song and the left side (the digital side) is engaged when you count.

The 9 Gamut Procedure is a 10 second process wherein 9 of these 'brain stimulating' actions are performed while continuously tapping on one of the body's energy points - the Gamut Point.

It has been found, after years of experience, that this routine can add efficiency to EFT and hastens your progress towards emotional freedom - especially when sandwiched between 2 trips through The Sequence.

One way to help memorize the Basic Recipe is to look at it as though it was a ham sandwich.

The Setup is the preparation for the ham sandwich - and the sandwich itself consists of two slices of bread (The Sequence) with the ham, or middle portion, as the 9 Gamut Procedure. It looks like this:

> *The Setup*
> *The Ham Sandwich:*   *The Sequence (Bread)*
> *9 Gamut (Ham)*
> *The Sequence (Bread)*

To do the 9 Gamut Procedure, you must first locate the Gamut Point. It is on the back of either hand and is 1/2 inch behind the midpoint between the knuckles at the base of the ring finger and the little finger.

If you draw an imaginary line between the knuckles at the base of the ring finger and little finger and consider that line to be the base of an equilateral triangle whose other sides converge to a point (apex) in the direction of the wrist, then the Gamut Point would be located at the apex of the triangle.

The 9 Gamut Actions

Next, you must perform 9 different actions while tapping the Gamut point continuously. These are:

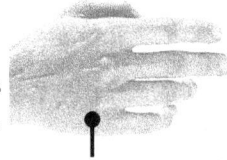

Gamut Point

1. *Eyes closed.*
2. *Eyes open.*
3. *Eyes hard down right while holding the head steady.*
4. *Eyes hard down left while holding the head steady.*
5. *Roll eyes in a circle as though your nose was at the center of a clock and you were trying to see all the numbers in order.*
6. *Same as #5 only reverse the direction in which you roll your eyes.*
7. *Hum 2 seconds of a song (suggest Happy Birthday).*
8. *Count rapidly from 1 to 5.*
9. *Hum 2 seconds of a song again.*

Note that these 9 actions are presented in a certain order and I suggest that you memorize them in the order given. However, you can mix the order up if you wish so long as you do all 9 of them - AND you perform 7, 8 and 9 as a unit.

That is, you hum 2 seconds of a song, then count, then hum the song again, in that order.

Years of experience have proven this to be most important.

Also, note that for some people humming Happy Birthday causes resistance because it brings up memories of unhappy birthdays.

In this case, you can either use EFT on those unhappy memories and resolve them - or you can side-step this issue for now by humming some other song.

The Sequence (again)

The fourth, and last, ingredient in the Basic Recipe is an identical repeat trip through The Sequence.

The Reminder Phrase

Once memorized, the Basic Recipe becomes a lifetime friend. It can be applied to an almost endless list of emotional and physical problems and provides relief from most of them.

However, there's one more concept we need to develop before we can apply the Basic Recipe to a given problem. It's called the Reminder Phrase.

When a football quarterback throws a pass he aims it at a particular receiver. He doesn't just throw the ball in the air and hope someone will catch it.

Likewise, the Basic Recipe needs to be aimed at a specific problem. Otherwise, it will bounce around aimlessly with little or no effect.

You 'aim' the Basic Recipe by applying it while 'tuned in' to the problem from which you want relief. This tells your system which problem needs to be the receiver.

You may remember the discovery statement: *"The cause of all negative emotions is a disruption in the body's energy system."*

Negative emotions come about because you are tuned into certain thoughts or circumstances which, in turn, cause your energy system to disrupt. Otherwise, you function normally.

One's fear of heights is not present, for example, while one is reading the comic section of the Sunday newspaper - and therefore not tuned in to the problem.

Tuning in to a problem can be done by simply thinking about it. In fact, tuning in means thinking about it !

Thinking about the problem will bring about the energy disruptions involved which then - and only then - can be balanced by applying the Basic Recipe.

Without tuning in to the problem, and thereby creating those energy disruptions, the Basic Recipe does nothing.

To tune in merely think about the problem while applying the Basic Recipe. That's it - at least in theory !

However, you may find it a bit difficult to consciously think about the problem while you are tapping, humming, counting, etc.

That's why we introduce a Reminder Phrase that you can repeat continually while you are performing the Basic Recipe.

The Reminder Phrase is simply a word or short phrase that describes the problem and that you repeat out loud each time you tap one of the points in The Sequence.

In this way you continually 'remind' your system about the problem you are working on.

The best Reminder Phrase to use is usually identical to what you choose for the affirmation you use in The Setup.

For example, if you are working on a fear of public speaking, The Setup affirmation would go like this:

> *"Even though I have this **fear of public speaking**.*
> *I deeply and completely accept myself"*

Within this affirmation, the underlined words *fear of public speaking* are ideal candidates for use as the Reminder Phrase - you could change this to something similar, such as *public speaking fear* or just *public speaking* instead of the somewhat longer version above.

Subsequent Round Adjustments

Let's say you are using the Basic Recipe for some problem - fear, headache, anger, etc.

Sometimes the problem will simply vanish after just one round while, at other times, one round provides only partial relief.

When only partial relief is obtained, you will need to do one or more additional rounds - and these subsequent rounds need to be adjusted slightly for best results.

One of the main reasons why the first round doesn't always completely eliminate a problem is because of the re-emergence of Psychological Reversal - that interfering blockage that The Setup is designed to correct.

This time, Psychological Reversal shows up in a somewhat different form !   Instead of blocking your progress altogether it now blocks any remaining progress !

You have already made some headway but become stopped part way toward complete relief because Psychological Reversal enters in a manner that keeps you from getting any better.

Since the subconscious mind tends to be very literal, the subsequent rounds of the Basic Recipe need to address the fact that you are working on the remaining problem.

Accordingly, the affirmation contained within The Setup needs to be adjusted - as does the Reminder Phrase.

Here's the adjusted format for The Setup affirmation:

> *"Even though I __still__ have __some__ [of the problem]*
> *I deeply and completely accept myself."*

Please note the emphasized words (still & some) and how they change the thrust of the affirmation toward the remainder of the problem.

It should be easy to make adjustments like this and, after a little experience, you will fall into it quite naturally.

Usage Comments

How Often Should EFT be Used ?

Whenever the need is felt - and in between ! Persistence pays !

If you do your EFT work at home, at work, at play - then you work in different environments, which may improve the efficiency of EFT.

Disposal of Unwanted Energies

Comment has been made by clairvoyants who use EFT about disposal of the energies that are released. They have reported that sometimes these 'hang around' and may 'get back in'.

So it is advisable to ask *"That all unwanted energies be taken to the best place for them and be Healed."*

There is Good in the Worst of Us,
And Bad in the Best of Us

Improving Our Performance

Each of us knows one person better than any other - our own self.

We are very aware of all our faults and our problems, and often tend to have a low opinion of ourselves, although we may put on a different face for others to see.

When we meet another person for the first time, it is usual to try to see the best in them; often we may envy their happiness, not realizing that they are worse off than ourselves.

We all have 'ups and downs' in life - the big difference is how we handle the 'downs'.

Life is Full of Lessons

We can choose to learn from the lessons that life gives to us, or we can spend our time complaining about them.

Many illustrious authors, such as Caroline Myss, have written how some very sick people just do not want to be healed.

They spend lots of their time going to Doctors and Healers, and say that they want to be Healed - but deep inside them the story is the opposite.

Perhaps they enjoy telling others of their woes, boasting that their sickness is beyond the skills of Doctor X, getting sympathy from their associates, or even using their illness as a means of getting attention or controlling the lives of family members.

Being a Victim

This attitude is not restricted to health. An individual or group of people may have suffered in various ways at the hand of others.

Any such suffering is to be deplored; but how an individual handles it can vary enormously. Many blame all their problems as the result of such suffering, refusing to take any responsibility even for problems that are not connected to the suffering.

Others realize that what has happened has happened, that it is in the past, and can not be allowed to spoil their life. These people have learnt a big lesson !

They are no longer victims - they have become victors. Victors over their natural 'poor me' attitude. They can get on and enjoy a good life - not forgetting the suffering, but knowing that it can be overcome.

Overcoming Anger

Anger and hate are not necessarily bad. You can hate an animal being mistreated, and have anger at the perpetuator. How you handle this anger is the most important aspect - for you.

Getting into a rage can just cause injury to yourself, and perhaps cause the perpetuator to 'take more' out on the poor animal to relieve the increased emotions that result.

Is it not better to act in a calm fashion to decide how you can act to stop the mistreatment and prevent such actions in the future ?

This may not be easy ! But your intent at self-control is itself a benefit for you - and you may be able to help the mistreated victim as well.

Let us imagine that a bully is beating a dog. What would happen if you take a few calming breaths, and then ask the bully about something completely unassociated with him or the dog, such as the best way to get somewhere ?

Hopefully you will not be told to 'go to hell', but succeed in breaking the chain of action. You may ask a few more similar questions, and perhaps then compliment the bully on having such a nice dog ! Even ask if you can pat him - the dog, not the bully !

The bully may then tell why the dog is bad - perhaps you may be able to suggest a way of training the dog to change its behaviour.

Discretion may be advisable. If you are male, and see a man beating his wife, it may be best not to compliment the man on having a pretty wife - and do not ask to pat (or kiss) her !

Asking questions that do not imply guilt is far better than telling someone that they are guilty - and more likely to change behaviour.

This is so in everyday life - when at home or at work. When you show positive interest in a person, you are more likely to get a positive response.

Holding on to Anger

When you have anger you hurt yourself. It is recognized as being a major contributor to Heart and liver problems.

Holding anger at someone with whom you work, among your associates, or in your family, is most disruptive for others as well - and will result in them doing their best to reduce your influence, so as to lessen the disruption.

This lowering of your influence (in whatever ways are relevant) will also reduce your influence in other ways, which may well reduce your benefits of being in that group. You lose !

When you hold anger at someone distant in place, or at a happening distant in time, you only hurt yourself - not them !

It is imperative to release all anger, hate, and similar negative emotions. Sometimes this can be most difficult - but it is still worthwhile.

Perhaps the most difficult cases involve rape - especially when this occurred incestuously to a young child. In many cases the trauma exists, yet without the knowledge being accessible to conscious memory.

When this is uncovered, or if it is known already, every device possible should be used to enable forgiveness. In many cases this type of hurting runs in families - the father may have suffered similar abuse as a child.

Even draw on the concept of karma, or that some unknown past life incidents may be involved. How does not matter so much as somehow finding the ability to forgive !

There are many instances of women being raped - and this memory is held with emotional triggers that prevent a normal life.

The incident has already happened - you are NOT going to reverse it. But you can accept that it happened and get on with your life. In some cases you may have even contributed in some way to the rape - look inside yourself and forgive yourself, too.

Self Destruction

We know ourselves better than we know any other person. This includes our faults and our problems. When we concentrate our thoughts on ourselves we tend to magnify these faults and problems.

Worrying occurs when we have identified a problem and then go round and round and round thinking of nothing else - except, perhaps, other problems to make matters worse.

This is self destruction - we are sabotaging ourselves.

What is the absolute very worst that can happen as a result of the problem ? How likely is this to happen ? In most cases, it is not likely at all !

Think of the people that you know - or have heard about. Are there any in a position worse than yours ? Did you get a meal yesterday ? Some people have not had a decent meal for many days. You may have shelter - many others do not.

So your situation is not all that bad. How can you improve it ? Be positive ! Some keys to help:

1. Define the problem clearly and precisely - write it down.
2. Identify the factors involved - who, why, when, where, how.
3. Decide if any other influences are pertinent, and their effect.
4. Think of ALL the possible ways to improve the situation.
5. Being realistic, consider which is the most workable way.
6. Plan in detail how you will implement this solution.
7. Do it ! Correctly !

When I first went to the Royal Military Academy, Sandhurst, the Regimental Sergeant Major in Charge explained that if we had decided to make the army a career, we obviously did not have the slightest idea of the thinking process.

Since we were there, to be trained as officers, it would be advantageous to the army if we did learn how to think - and these were the keys that were taught to us.

It was also explained throughout our training that proper implementation was essential.

There were many examples given where excellent implementation of the not-best plan succeeded, whilst the best plan failed when not implemented correctly.

Happiness

Since we know our own faults so well, we find it difficult to be happy about ourselves - or happy in other ways.

The real key to happiness is not to think of ourselves, except to think how we can help others.

This does not mean that we neglect ourselves, since we need to be fit and healthy to be able to do a good job of helping others.

When we help others, we get a great sense of satisfaction - we have 'done good'.   And we often find that we get helped ourselves in various ways - not just by those that we helped, but from sources and in ways that we do not expect.

On occasion we may find a person that does not want to be helped. Respect their decision, and do not intrude on their misery.   They may have lessons to learn, or enjoy being miserable !

There are always others who we can help - so why waste time and effort where it it is not wanted ?

When I lived in Jamaica, a fellow yachtsman took the trouble to tell me that I was drinking far too much and making a fool of myself. I recognized that this took a lot of effort on his part, and showed care - so I listened and took his advice, knowing that he was a real friend.

Joy

Being joyful is different from just being happy - it is a far deeper emotion.

Pete Sanders has written a book 'Access your Brain's Joy Center' in which he describes how the area around the pituitary and pineal glands controls your mood.

Pete instructs how to use your hands to locate and enliven this 'Joy Center'. He warns, however, that if you are too low then you can 'stir up' the reptilian part of your brain with the opposite results.

I have found that I do not need my hands.   My 'awareness' intuitively knows where to go, and by sending my awareness to this place and making clockwise circles of the 'Joy Center' I can achieve the result of releasing any negative mood.

This is done with a clockwise movement as perceived when imagining that you are looking down onto your head - passing left to right as you go in front, front to rear on your right side, right to left at the rear, and rear to front on your left side.

For best results, always avoid counter-clockwise movements unless you are intentionally extracting something - as will be explained in later chapters.

Pete explains in his book how this can be of great assistance in working with anger, depression, rejection, and addictions.

This could be a very useful extension of the 'Emotional Freedom Techniques' previously mentioned - they are not mutually exclusive, they actually complement each other.

Sing a Happy Song

There have been many times in my life when I felt deeply depressed and very sad. One way that I found to overcome this mood was to sing a happy song:

> *I'm Happy, Happy, - Happy all day long*
> *I'm Happy, Happy singing this song.*
> *I'm Happy, Happy, - Happy as can be*
> *I'm Happy, Happy singing merrily.*

Remember to sing it to a bright and happy tune - not a dirge ! If in company, you can sing it quietly to yourself, inside you head.

I found it impossible to remain sad and depressed when my reality was that I was singing a happy song !

Try it next time you feel sad or depressed - you may find that it works for you, too ! And it is free ! No doctors prescriptions are needed. No pills to take which may have side effects.

Laughter is Infectious

This is along the same lines. Laughter has been described as the world's best medicine, and there is that old saying:

> *Laugh and the world laughs with you.*
> *Cry, and you cry alone.*

But always remember - laugh <u>with</u> other people, not <u>at</u> other people.

If they are sad, perhaps you can help them see the funny side of their troubles, the silver lining to their clouds.

Random Acts of Kindness

No matter how small, the intent is the same - to help another person.   If you do this just for your own ego, forget it; the intent to help the other person must be paramount - yes, you will feel good, but this should not be the aim.

Perhaps it is better to give long-lasting help, rather than just a temporary fix - like giving a fishing hook and teaching them how to catch fish, rather than giving them a fish to eat.

Help others to help themselves.   Sometimes they may be in dire circumstances and need immediate assistance, and this should be given to the best of your abilities - to help them get on their own feet again.

But beware of those who go from one person to another, asking help, getting it, but never helping themselves; and do not let your family suffer unduly in giving help, except in a real emergency.

Respect and Love

As we grow, our influence grows - similar to the way that ripples in a pond go out to cover the whole pond.

We start with our own self, then our family, next our community, perhaps our country, even the whole world.

One person's idea can change the course of history - like Florence Nightingale's efforts, resulting in wide-spread nursing; the Wright Brothers getting a flying machine to work; Marconi sending messages across the ocean; and many other examples.

Many people often forget that the Holy Creator did not just make humans, but all creatures.   Perhaps God is not just the God of humans, but also of the animals, plants, insects, and bacteria.

It may be that we should show respect for, and give love to, all the creations made by the Holy Creator - and not treat nature as just being there for our own convenience.

ABOU BEN ADAM - Son of Adam

Abou ben Adam, may his tribe increase
Awoke one night from a dream of peace
And saw in the moonlight of his room -
Making it rich, like a lily in bloom -
An Angel writing in a book of gold.
Exceeding peace made Ben Adam bold
To the presence in the room he said
"What writest thou ?" - The Angel raised his head
And replied, with a look of sweet accord,
"The names of those who Love the Lord".
"And is mine one ?" spoke Abou. "Nay, not so"
Replied the vision. Abou spoke more low,
But cheerily still, and said: "I pray thee, then,
Write me as one who loves his fellow men"
The Angel wrote and vanished. The next night
It came again with a great waking Light
And showed the names whom Love of God had Blessed.
Lo ! Ben Adam's name led all the rest.

Think of the Unemployment that would Ensue
If All Health were Perfect - What would we Do ?

Illness

Let us define illness as any condition of our Being that results in a dis-ease effect on our physical body - since that is when we know that something is wrong.

Dis-ease is just that - not 'at ease', the vibrational patterns of some parts of us are stressed beyond limits, our body cannot cope with what is happening, signals to us that there is a major problem, and that action is needed to deal with this stress.

Most of the Western medical concepts are primarily concerned with overcoming the symptoms - cancelling the signals that are given and manifest in the physical body.

Most of the modern day pharmaceutical medicines have been derived from plants - the same plants that were used by ancient 'medicine men' (and often women) and are now used by homeopaths and herbalists.

There is great opposition from the pharmaceutical companies against those who use the natural medicines in their original state; 'purity' of manufacture is claimed, yet these made medicines have been shown to have many side effects that do not occur with the plants when used naturally by those who understand them.

Perhaps this is due to the pharmaceutical companies dealing with medicines as just a chemical soup - they deal with the 'dead' chemical constituents, ignoring the Life Force that is in the natural plant. Anyway, they can sell more medicines to deal with the side effects - more profit !

Most medical doctors choose that career because they wish to be Healers; at medical school they learn about the physical body and how to recognize symptoms of illness. Then they are taught only which pharmaceutical medicines to prescribe !

Let us recognize that the pharmaceutical companies have a massive influence on western medicine - they have their profits to maintain ! They give grants to medical schools, free samples to doctors, advertising revenue to professional journals, and funding to the medical associations.

Governmental staff, who are supposed to safeguard the national health, are often 'guided' by the drug companies - and the senior people later may be found lucratively employed by these same drug companies.

Research that is submitted to obtain permission to sell drugs is usually done by university researchers, the cost of research being subsidized by the pharmaceutical companies.

If the result is not beneficial to the pharmaceutical companies, it usually is not submitted to the authorities - and the research establishments involved may suffer a reduction in funding.

There are instances when cures are determined, yet tests cannot be funded - money is not made available for a simple reason: the treatment cannot be patented, so profits will not accrue to the drug companies.

Yes, there are many researchers who want to do a good job - but research is expensive, and they have families to house, feed and clothe. But the corporate mentality that is prevalent nowadays, including in universities, is geared to money. A change would be beneficial to all !

We have seen that the Human Being is far more than just a physical body - yet these other aspects are mostly ignored in western medical practice.

For good health, all aspects need to be considered.

Injury

The one form of illness that is primarily physical is injury - breaking a limb, or damaging flesh and skin by tearing, burning, or other similar calamities.

Let us be thankful for the skills of the surgeons who work on these problems, and for the advances in their knowledge.

In past times it was the barber who cut off a damaged limb, perhaps with the help of the blacksmith to sear the cut end. This was not always successful, since germs were not acknowledged, and there was not any attempt to maintain a clean environment.

Ridicule was poured on those who first realized that germs existed - they were vindicated only when microscopes were invented and germs could be seen.

Germs

The smallest of these are viruses - like sub-sections of DNA that infiltrate a cell, change its DNA, and replicate. These are indeed life forms ! They have the intelligence and knowledge to do their job - even after centuries of freezing in space.

Some even establish miniature factories within a cell, each one making a component - when ready, these are assembled and put into action.

The purpose of a virus is to effect change. Perhaps they have played a key role in evolution of our species. But generally our bodies do not like change, so the result is usually harmful to us.

Bacteria are far larger than viruses - many within us are beneficial to us; they are needed to help consume food and recycle unwanted cells, such as those that have been injured or died a natural death.

There are quite a few that are not so beneficial - or are doing their job in the wrong place or in an incorrect way.

Bacteria are needed to purify rivers - many of these consume oxygen, just like us. Generally bacteria that consume oxygen are beneficial, while those that do not consume oxygen do their work in different ways.

This can be observed in a rubbish pile - if it has plenty of air, then we do not smell bad fumes. Without such ventilation, it stinks.

The one thing that is common to both viruses and non-beneficial bacteria is that they like to multiply in a poor environment. If a person is in excellent health, then they are less likely to be the subject of a successful attack.

This can be described in another way - if your Life Force is strong, action is not needed by viruses or bacteria to correct the situation.

There are some viruses which will attack anyway - perhaps they are nature's assistants in keeping the human population within limits acceptable to the rest of nature; to prevent any human population explosion that results in a plague of humans - that devours all the resources of nature, to the detriment of other life forms.

This, of course, leads to the NIMBY syndrome - 'Not In My Back Yard', meaning take somebody else, not me, or my family (except, of course, my mother-in-law !).

The best defence is to keep healthy - which includes having a healthy diet.

To put this in perspective, statistics show that the world's population has grown by about 2,500 million since 1950; from 5,000 million to 7,500 million - a 50% increase.

By 2050 it may well reach 10,000 million, most of this increase coming in the lesser developed countries.

'We Are What We Eat'

- And drink, such as 'Diet Drinks' using aspartame which have been shown to have poisonous effects (to humans, not the bottom line of the drink makers).

'The Ecologist' reports that aspartame was listed by the Pentagon as a biochemical warfare agent. Today it's an integral part of the modern diet. Sold commercially under names like NutraSweet and Canderel, aspartame can be found in more than 5,000 foods.

Independent scientists say aspartame can produce a range of disturbing adverse effects in humans, including headaches, memory loss, mood swings, seizures, multiple sclerosis and Parkinson's-like symptoms, tumours and even death. It may be the cause of Attention Deficiency in many children - leading to Prozac drugging.

Aspartame now accounts for the majority (75 per cent) of all the complaints in the US adverse-reaction monitoring system.

So many foods on grocery shelves have additives to prolong shelf life - and this is especially so when it is a manufactured food.

These are not natural - and our bodies have been designed to consume natural foods. Even raw foods have often been poisoned by the pesticides and herbicides used by farmers - including farming corporations.

Fast Food outlets get a lot of disparagement; some of this is deserved, since many of the animals that are 'used' are stuffed with anti-biotics, maltreated during their life, and killed without dignity.

This also applies to most meat products in shops, however.

Traces of these pesticides, herbicides, and anti-biotics accumulate in our bodies - and can prove very troublesome as this accumulation grows.

Suppose we become vegetarians - would this help ? Many believe so, but studies have shown that humans need some vitamins, etc., that can only come from consuming animal matter.

It has also been accepted that the types of humans differ - some need a strong meat diet, whilst others can thrive on lesser amounts.

Our bodies need many nutrients for good health - especially vitamins and trace minerals. A food product may look attractive on the store shelves, but be of little or no nutritional value.

Mark Purdey has investigated 'Mad Cow' disease. He has found this to be quite widespread among wild deer and other animals in areas where there has been little human contact.

These animals have not been fed any recycled animal foods, which have been accepted by most governmental authorities as being the cause of 'Mad Cow' disease.

But there is one common denominator - high manganese and low copper content of the soils; this means that the grasses that grow, though they look fine to the animals, do not give them all the needed minerals There are many trace minerals that we need for good health. See Nexus Magazine: Vol 10 nos 3 & 4 - the web site is www.nexusmagazine.com

There is a very strong case for consuming 'organic' produce - food that is not subjected to chemicals, but uses natural fertilizers from plants recycled by Mother Nature; by eating meat and eggs from animals and chickens that roam free, not penned in tiny cages - or stuffed with anti-biotics.

Unfortunately the pesticides and herbicides that are used by many farmers kill many of the bacteria and enzymes within the soil, so reducing its ability to regenerate.

Insects that are killed are then eaten by birds and other insects, and they lose their own good health. In 2007 there are reports that the bee population in parts of Europe and the USA are not surviving - which may prevent pollination of plants and so cause a great shortage of vegetables and fruit.

These poisons are washed into streams, ponds, rivers, lakes, seas and oceans.   Warnings have been issued about restricting the amount of salmon consumed - they range the oceans and they have been found to be contaminated by the poisons (including industrial wastes) dumped by people in 'civilized' countries.

Perhaps one of the best ways to ensure that you have good food is to grow as much as you can yourself. In England, during the 1939-45 war, dollars and shipping could not be spared to import food - and much was sunk by U-boat action.

So people grew food in their own gardens, or they obtained 'allotments' (small pieces of land where they could grow their own plants) if they lacked gardens. This helped the Brits to survive - and maintain good health. It gave them extra food over and above their rations.

This system still exists, and is common in many parts of Europe. Sometimes the quality of soil may be very poor, not normally able to grow much, as was the case with Findhorn in Scotland.

By making a concentrated effort to work with nature, showing respect to the land and giving love to the plants, good crops were grown both at Findhorn (a desert-like barren spot) and at Perelandra in the USA. See www.findhorn.org & www.perelandra-ltd.com

From Siberia comes the wonderful story of Mind working with nature to help the Russian people to grow good food on small lots - and this has succeeded to the extent that a considerable portion of the Russian food requirements is now grown by 'Dachniks' in miniature Dachas - and is of excellent quality.

This story is told in a series of books about the 'Ringing Cedars of Russia' - the website www.RingingCedars.com has more details.

Life Force in Food

It may be that Love is the real 'Life Force' throughout nature; and when we give love to plants they respond by doing their best to help us. But it is so easy to kill this life force by overcooking - raw food is usually best for us, although digestion may not always be so easy !

One of the most sure ways to kill this life force is by 'microwaving' food. Microwaves work by moving the cellular parts of a food extremely quickly, similar but far more intense than the increased speed of cells resulting from heating them.

Independent research by Dr Hans Hertel in Switzerland first identified and quantified this problem - the corporations went to extreme lengths to stop the publication of the results. To see more details look at: www.mercola.com/article/microwave/hazards2.htm and www.relfe.com/microwave.html

I was brought up in a strict religion where food was always blessed. I rebelled against the narrow-mindedness of this group, and so also abandoned their procedures - including the blessing of food.

When I learnt how to locate auras, I experimented on the food that I ate. With blessing, the aura of food doubles in size ! Since this indicates an increased life force having more love, I now bless all that I consume.

Pains that Move

Those who studied science at school may remember one of the major differences between solids and liquids and gases.

With both solids and liquids, if you place one into another by immersion or mixing, the volume to hold these is the same as before such mixing. Put a stone into a jar of water, and the level of water rises to accommodate the volume of the stone.

But you can have a container full of one gas and then pour the same volume of a different gas into the same container without spillage - the molecules of one gas fit into the spaces between the molecules of the other gas.

It may be that life forms in different dimensions can so occupy the same space in a similar fashion.

Many people who can see the auras of other persons report that there are different auras, the more dense being smaller and closer to the physical body.

They also report that the less dense auras interpenetrate those that are more dense.

Is it possible that other life forms, operating at less dense vibrational patterns than our physical bodies, can exist inside our bodies ?

Since these other life forms are foreign to us, it would be understandable that we felt them as a pain; they could interfere with our own vibrational patterns, and we would feel the result.

Have you ever had a pain that seems to move around in you ? What did your doctor do to free you from this pain ? Aspirin and similar pain relieving medicines may alleviate the pain by deadening your feelings - but was the pain completely removed ?

Perhaps there is a case for the help of Spiritual Healers and Clairvoyants - they may be able to see the cause of such pains and take the needed action for removal.

Earth Energies

Talking to many members of the medical profession in North America about noxious earth energies is similar to going back in time a few hundred years and telling people about radio waves, or their barber-surgeons about germs.

Just because people do not believe in something does not mean that it does not exist, or that they will not be affected. This is rather like an ostrich burying its head so it cannot see a predator.

If we accept that everything is energy in various forms, including ourselves, then we should accept that other energies can have an effect on our well-being - even those that we cannot see, that operate in different dimensions but have an effect in the physical.

Because these energies have such an effect upon us, upon our bodies, we can use this sensitivity of our body to locate energies - especially those that operate in distinct 'energy bands' that differ from the surrounding background energies.

When we have knowledge of these and tune our minds to them, we can feel these energy bands with our hands - experience is needed for the best results.

One form of such energy is the electro-magnetic force emanating from cathode ray tubes used in television and computer screens.

As an experiment, keep a thought of these energy emissions and approach the area in front of your TV screen from the side, holding one of your hands in front of you with its palm facing forwards.

Can you feel any slight difference as you move forward ? You may find that the air seems slightly more dense as you move towards the area right in front of the screen.

If you repeat this at a distance further from the TV, the effect can still be felt, but not as strongly.

If you can feel this energy with your hands, be sure that the organs within your body that find this energy to be detrimental will be even more sensitive to the energy.

Most of the earth energies seem to be in vertical bands - they effect a penthouse suite just as much as a basement apartment. When two bands cross, a vortex is formed, which has an even more detrimental effect on the energies of your own body.

In Europe there have been numerous researches made by medical doctors concerning 'cancer homes'.

These researches have shown that there are distinct housing areas and places within homes that are subject to 'earth energies' that are noxious to humans - and to most animals and plants.

The investigation of these noxious energies was revived in modern times by Gustav Baron von Pohl, and by medical doctors such as Drs Curry and Hartmann in Germany. Studies were made of where noxious energies existed, were plotted on maps, and then compared with deaths from cancer - with excellent correlation.

As a result there are places in Europe where geopathic studies are required before hospitals, schools, and other institutions are built. Käthe Bachler of Austria conducted a study of over 11,000 people in 14 countries and 3,000 homes - cases where extended sitting or sleeping caused sudden infant deaths, inattention at school, and diseases such as cancer, arthritis, and heart problems.

In all these cases it needed only to change the position of the seat or bed to avoid bad spots - and when this was done the health problems disappeared !

About 25% of deaths in North America are cancer related (2007 estimate now 33%). The incidence of cancer in gypsies is low - in a survey less than 2% had any relative that had died from cancer.

The gypsies (and probably most aboriginal people) seldom stay in any one place for an extended period, may be more Intuitive about noxious energies, and are aware of places to avoid.

Examples from Käthe Bachler's book 'Earth Radiation'

Case# 264. Anita, 10 years old, told me: *"I have been sleeping in this room for the past year. I sleep poorly, I am so tired in the morning, and I have headaches most of the time".*

Change of bed ! After only three days she reports happily: *"Now I sleep very well and feel well. And I am so happy, because I am finally warm in bed. Before my bed was moved, I was always so cold in bed".*

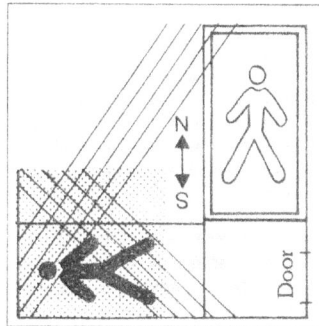

Case# 1507b. Ingebord had two places for doing homework.

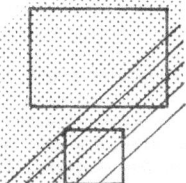

Place 1 does not feel well, short concentration span.

Place 2 feels well and cheerful, does extra work for credit.

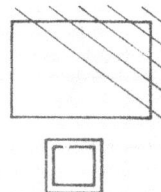

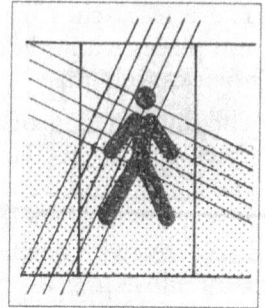

Case# 164. After her grandfather's death (he had died six months earlier from lung cancer), Lotte was given the privilege of sleeping in her grandfather's old bed.

She immediately lost her appetite, suffered from headaches, had trouble sleeping and lost many days from school.

As soon as the bed was moved to another location, she felt better again.

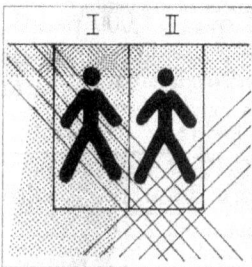

Case# 987. Mr. LL has multiple sclerosis.

Mrs. H. from Salzburg asked for an examination. Afterwards I asked her which bed her husband was sleeping in.

She said: *"In this one"*, and pointed to bed II. I looked surprised and she explained that he had been sleeping in bed I for 7 years and that they had changed beds only two weeks ago.

I recommended a different place.

Case# 610. Premature birth.

Gall bladder, cramps, and pain in the feet, premature delivery.

The doctor believed that without the appropriate measures, the foetus would have been aborted.

The dowser said: *"The child wanted to flee from the uteris."*

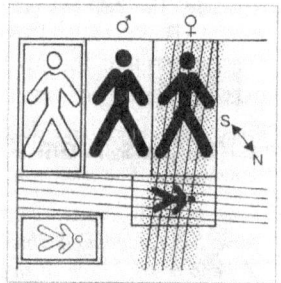

The child was born after 6½ months of pregnancy, cried most of the time, had convulsions, was restless.

The mother had to getup at night as often as 20 times to quiet the baby.

After the bed was moved to another place, there was improvement.

Case# 660. The ten-month-old baby was tied to his crib.

The parents were afraid he might fall out of bed, because he stood up again and again.

When in his playpen, he only occupied the half which was 'free of radiation', never the half above the Curry Line.

The father finally phoned me: *"Since we moved the bed, we have had no problem with his sleeping and he is healthy and robust."*

Case# 201. School psychologist was puzzled.

During the first and second year of the child's life, his development seemed retarded, and he did not talk at all.

During the third to sixth year of life, the child was classified as mentally retarded.

The school psychologist's judgement was *"This child needs to be put into a school for the handicapped."*

Through sheer coincidence, the child's bed was moved - and suddenly all the effort and care of his intelligent mother brought measurable success.

The child progressed in all areas of his life.

He was put into a regular grammar school on a trial basis. To everyone's surprise, he came home with 'Good' on his first report card.

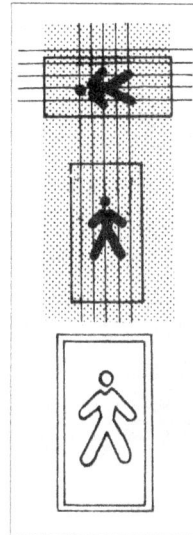

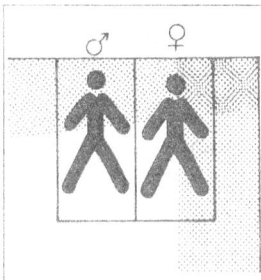

Case# 81. Migraine

The couple lived in a room for 18 months. He felt constantly 'under the weather'. She suffered from severe migraines, insomnia, and many other complaints.

A letter from them reported rapid improvement as soon as their bed was moved to another place.

Case# 510. Cramps in the legs

Mrs. R. suffered from cramps in the legs almost every night, and also from insomnia, duodenal ulcer, and phlebitis.

Four months after moving her bed she wrote: *"What a blessing to be able to sleep through the night. Ever since I rearranged the bed, I have had neither pains nor cramps in the legs."*

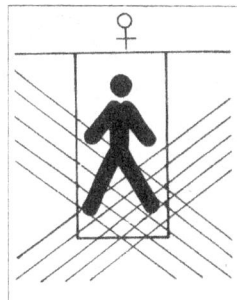

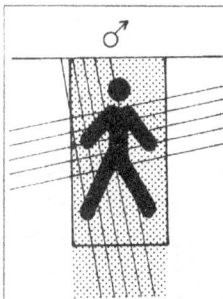

Case# 565. Stomach cancer

was the cause of death of Mr. L. three years after he moved into this house; his son's bed is located exactly beneath his on the floor below - he too suffers from severe stomach ailments, swelling of the lymph nodes, and abscesses over much of his body. The doctor had tried to help for years, but to no avail, and a thorough examination in the hospital did not shed light on the disease.

Only after the bed was moved could the medication work and the patient became well.

Is your Bed Safe ?

One way to check if your bed or chair is in a zone of noxious energy is to keep a thought of 'noxious energy' in your Heart-Mind-Brain team, and feel for any changes 'in the air' around your bed or chair.

You do not have to be an expert of noxious energy to do this - your body is very aware of any noxious effect !

Another way is to stand at the foot of your bed, or in front of your chair (home or office), and ask your Heart *"Is there any energy zone on any part of my bed (or chair) that is noxious to me ?"*

You can also quantify any of these noxious energies, by asking *"Is this noxious energy causing illness to me ?"* remembering that although your body may have reserves to overcome the effect, those reserves are not limitless - so the noxious energy may have a bad effect that worsens as time progresses.

Disease may result quickly in an environment of strong noxious energy, or may manifest over a number of years where they are weaker.

If you usually lie down in a way that avoids a particular area of your bed, or fail to wake up feeling refreshed, take this as a warning that your bed may be in a bad location - and check for noxious energies.

Also these 'drawdowns' of your reserves are cumulative; if you have bad positions for your bed and for any other place where you remain for a considerable time, then the combined drawdown may exceed your ability for replenishment.

If your body sways forward to give a YES signal, then imagine that your bed or chair is in another position, and repeat the question for that location. Imagine different locations until you find one that is free of noxious energy.

Now you may still have a problem - if your partner sleeps with you, s/he may still be in a zone of noxious energy, although you would be free ! So repeat this same exercise asking about your partner - hopefully finding a position that is safe for you both.

For your children and your other relations, do this exercise again remembering to substitute their name in the question asked.

Later we will examine some proven methods of locating, identifying, and quantifying noxious energies, and ways to work with these energies to reduce or eliminate their noxiousness - without having to move the bed or chair.

German New Medicine

Dr Ryke Geerd Hamer has made a most interesting discovery - that when there is any illness in the body, a CAT scan of the brain shows distinctive patterns at spots corresponding to the site of the illness, and that these patterns change with variations of the stage of the illness.

He questioned patients who were suffering from serious diseases, and ascertained that in almost every case the patient had been traumatized to some extent just before the onset of the disease.

Dr Hamer postulates that these are connected - similar to the 'fight or flight' reaction that is well recognized, but being of a far longer time span.   He suggests that the sub-conscious takes what it understands (perhaps incorrectly !) to be the needed corrective action - and that this is recognized by us as an illness.

He explains that if the trauma is overcome, then this reaction moves to a healing mode.   Failing this, an even more serious illness or death may occur.   The longer that the trauma remains active, the more difficult is recovery to good health.

This makes sense !   It is an excellent reason for a person to take precautions against being traumatized - and if this does occur, to take action to negate the effects.

This means that the events causing trauma must be recognized as potential threats to our own good health.   Trauma is essentially emotional, and taking action such as the 'Emotional Freedom Techniques' (EFT) can be a great help in releasing such causes of future illness.

Typical traumatic experiences include:
...   Loss of a friend, relative, associate, or pet.
...   Relationship problems at home or at work.
...   Loss of employment or failure to be promoted.
...   Injury to a person that you love or feel responsibility.
...   Recognizing that you hurt another in some way.
...   Anger at behavior of others.
...   Worries about ourselves or others.

In many cases like these the traumatic event has already happened - there is nothing that we can do to change the event, but we can change our own re-action to the event.

Recognition of a trauma, and that it can cause ill-health to our own self is sometimes difficult - we lose a close relation, and are so upset that we do not realize that we are hurting ourselves !

Would it not be better to just be thankful for the experience that you have had with the deceased, wish them well in their next existence, and get on with your own life ?

You may have been left in a financial mess in this way, or find problems in 'carrying on'. Do not worry about these - just know that the situation could be far worse, that other people have gone through similar times and survived, and that somehow or other things will be fine in the end.

Do your best, and remember that you can always ask the help of 'Upstairs' !

Dr Hamer further proposes that most of what the medical profession sees as illness is, in fact, part of the Healing process. His propositions can only be described as turning medical practice 'upside down' - and so the medical authorities are rather incensed !

If Dr Hamer is correct, then the medicines produced by the drug companies would not be needed - and the potential loss of these profits is certainly stirring action to ridicule his findings.

This, of course, is the typical reaction of 'the Establishment' to any new thought that threatens those that are now 'in Power'.

Historically the medical profession is a prime example - witness the reaction to the theory that sterilization of surgical tools would reduce sickness, the battle waged against Radionics, and the persecution of Dr Rife.

If you would like more information on Dr Hamer's work, see www.GermanNewMedicine.ca - it is not easy reading, but is worthwhile !

The **key point** is that we must recognize traumatic events as potentially disease causing to our own selves, and take action to protect ourselves - including to use EFT, which costs nothing except our own time and effort, cannot cause any harm, and has a proven track record.

There are Those that Love 'Being Ill'
To get Compassion, Control Others Will !

Simple Healing

We are all Energy Beings - and since we are 'All the Same' we can help each other. Some things are easy for us to do - and some almost impossible (for us !).

But these 'almost impossible' things may be quite easy for those 'Upstairs' to do, using 'God Level' resources that we may lack. And the converse is true - we may have abilities in the physical plane that are not directly available to 'Upstairs'.

When we work together as a team, all things may be possible !

If our ego is in control, then teamwork may be very difficult; with our Heart in command, co-operation becomes relatively easy.

This is, perhaps, the biggest and most important skill in Healing - to know (and accept) that we do not give Healing ourselves, but act (like a conduit) as a link for the 'Healing Energies' from 'Upstairs' to go and help another Being.

These Healing Energies are attracted when you have the intent to help another - not for reward, but because it is 'the best way to Be', to want to assist others for good purposes.

This does not mean that a professional Healer should not charge for their own time - they have to feed, clothe, and house their families, and perhaps pay rent, staff and travel expenses.

The problem comes when their fees are excessive, when they are charging for the help given by 'Upstairs', not just for their own expenses.

In this discussion, you will be the 'Healer', and the other person who is being Healed we will call the 'Healee'.

Protection

There are many reports of people who do Healing getting hurt themselves.

Before doing any Healing work, always clear and protect yourself. Ask 'Upstairs' or 'The System' to protect you.

A simple way is:

> *"I ask The System to clear from me all negativity*
> *And to protect me in this Healing work,*
> *To enclose both myself and the Healee in Light and Love.*
> *Let nothing that is not mine come to me;*
> *Let nothing that is not their own go to the Healee;*
> *Except the Light, Love, and Healing from 'Upstairs'.*
> *As I work to Heal others, let myself be Healed as well.*
> *All Healing to be without harm to others.*
> *I send you my gratitude and my Love"*

Another aspect which, unfortunately, is not generally recognized is that there are many energies, other dimensional life forms, that have themselves been hurt, perhaps by being given bad jobs that they do not like - such as being involved in anger or hate.

These energies that have been hurt seek Healing for themselves; when they find a Healer who is actively working to Heal others, they may come for Healing themselves.

The Healer in many cases does not understand this, feeling the effect of these energies as being detrimental, and telling them *"Go to the ends of the universe and never trouble any Being again"*.

This is like you going to a doctor and being told to 'F... Off' !

It is so simple to help them, and it costs you nothing. Just ask the 'Force for Good' to come and take them to be Healed, so that they can again be 'In the Light' and in their rightful place.

When you do this, you may be extremely surprised at how the atmosphere around you improves - do it often !

Grounding

We stand upright between the earth and the sky; and there is a voltage difference (perhaps small) with change of height. This is measurable in the physical dimension - and also effects the other dimensions. They need to be 'Grounded' as well !

It is well known that if a person keeps his 'Head in the Air' without being 'Down to Earth' problems arise in many ways. These may include energy patterns in and around our body, and may contribute to poor health.

As explained before, thoughts are perceived as 'Real Things' in the other dimensions; these (and other energy patterns) can find release if you are 'Grounded'.

How do you do this ? Just imagine that you have roots that extend from your body down into the earth - just like a tree ! Sound ridiculous, perhaps - but it works !

So imagine that you have roots growing from your feet and the base of your spine, and that these move with you - to connect you to 'Mother Earth'.

Being 'imaginary' these roots go straight through carpets, floors, concrete foundations, and all things that would prevent or disrupt connections in the physical world.

Washing Machine

This is a very simple method that does not require any medical knowledge, just good intent and lots of Love.

It was developed by Joe and Marta Smith, a farming couple from Nebraska, and has been used by them (and by many others) with great success.

This is how Joe tells about this wonderful system:

Hands-on Healing is a good way to help others. I'll take you through the method I like to use when possible.

To do this you should have 2 people and practice on each other. You will be the 'Healer', and the other person the 'Healee'.

For the Healee, get your partner or a close friend that you always drink coffee with and doesn't think you're completely nuts but will humour you.

Step 1: Set the Healee in a chair right in front of you. During all this exercise both you and the Healee should breathe in through your nose and exhale out of your mouth. It also helps if you both take 3 'Pranic Breaths' to start - feeling the energy at the top of your nose as you inhale.

Step 2: You take a step back and say something nice to the Angels who you are going to work with you and send through you the Healing Energies that are needed.

God has all these Angels up there that love to help you do this Healing if you just call on them - so get serious, look up to the Heavens, and tell them how grateful you are for them being able and willing to help you.

Don't kid your self into believing that you alone are doing this. This power comes from somewhere else !

Step 3: Now ask the Angels to send the Healing Energies down into a spot right in front of you and just behind the Healee. As they do this, step into this spot with your elbows at your side and your hands ahead of you, the palms turned up to receive this energy. Feel the warmth and love coming into your whole body.

Step 4: Ask the Healee if it is alright if you touch him - or her, as the case may be. Walk up behind them and place your hands on their shoulders, sending God's love into his/her body.

You may find that sending 'Blessing 995' and 'Healing 997' with God's Love help it to work better - these have been found to work well, for some undetermined reason.

Stand there for a while feeling the power flow through your hands into the Healee.

Ask the Healee to visualize that his/her body is a washing machine and you are sending God's love in the form of a warm cleansing soap to cleanse their body of all the hurts and pains of their life.

"To cleanse all the fears, all the disappointments, all the 'shoulds' and 'should nots', animosities for others, and add forgiveness for those who have animosity toward you."

Throw anything else in there as you are guided - things that come to your mind that need clearing. You know this work is using Intuition, so add to or take off what you want, as your Intuition guides you to do.

Now back to the washing machine; take your index finger and apply light pressure to the front of the Healee's body just below the collar bone. This is where you send Healing Power to the Heart.

Do this for several minutes, or until you get the signal that the job is done. You will know !

Then using your thumbs, press slightly on their back 2 inches above the shoulder blade and 2 inches from each side of the spine - these are 'release points'.

As you do this, tell the Healee *"spin out all this stuff that has been bothering you for years. Spin it out just like a giant washing machine."*

As you are talking about all their problems you may feel them tighten up, and as they spin it out, they seem to just let it all loose and relax. If they are still a little tight ask them to spin it again - that you don't think they got it all out the first time.

If they need it, do the process again and send in more of God's warm love. Sometimes it takes several sessions to get the relief that the subject needs.

Step 5: You now fluff their aura just like you would a pillow - only don't hit the Healee; this is like putting the clothes in the dryer ! As you try this, you may feel the aura push back so very gently and lightly.

When you fluff their aura, you disperse any old, unwanted energy that is hanging around, just like the breeze taking away dampness on clothes hung on a line to dry.

Step 6: Often clothes look better when they are ironed; to do this put your hands in front of you, and with your palms facing each other bring them almost together several times - the air between your hands seems to get thicker, more 'bouncy'.

So do this motion, standing sideways to the Healee, bouncing the aura all the way down on one side, then the body itself, then go the other side and bounce that side.

You can stand in front and back, too, to bounce the aura from side to side, doing it in front, around the body, and the back.

Step 7: Another thing you can do is to 'fold the clothes' - move your hands over their body noticing any area that feels either hot or cold. This works best if they are on a massage table.

As you move across the area of an injury, or a diseased area, it will give off heat into the palm of your hand. It will feel like a warm breath of air, very subtle.

Ask the Angels to change any 'not good' energies in these places with Love so that all the energies in these places are beneficial.

Step 8: Most important - ask the Healee to join with you in sending Thanks, Gratitude, and Love to 'All who helped in this Healing'.

Even Angels get excited when their help is appreciated - and they may queue up to help you when needed !

Joe tells more:

"An example of heavenly help happened to me in Georgia one night. A lady came over to the place where we were staying and wanted me to work on her - using 'hands on' Healing.

She had a real bad case of shingles in the face - her face was badly swollen, especially the left side. So I took her to one of the bedrooms, sat her on a dressing stool, and did the Healing work.

After I got through I let her sit there for a while and 'come back to earth'.

As it turned out I wasn't kidding. She said that she had an 'out of body' experience while I was doing the healing.

As she was floating in the ceiling she looked down and saw herself being worked on by an angel, a big white angel - I wasn't even there ! These were her words, not mine."

Healing in General

It is necessary that you have the permission and co-operation of any person that you may help with Healing. The Washing Machine is a good example - you are asking the Healee to release 'not good' energies themselves, to release their own problems.

If they hang onto their anger, hate, etc. and refuse to release it, then they will not get the full benefit of Healing. Yet these 'negative emotions' seem to be the cause of much illness.

The Angelic Forces will not over-ride the 'Free Will' of people - if a person decides that they will not release it, there is not much that any Healer can do.

Cases where you may not be able to get the conscious permission of a Being that needs Healing include babies and small children, those who are unconscious for any reason, animals and plants.

In this case you can still ask the Angelic Forces for their help, but ensure that you ask that it 'be in the highest and best good' of the Healee.

Note that the term 'Angelic Forces' may be better than 'Angels', since these are labels that we apply, and the Healing may need help from Beings who may be different from Angels - but still members of the 'Force for Good'.

Even the most knowledgeable medical practitioners and Healers may not know exactly the best type of Healing that is needed; they may have a good idea, but use general terminology - perhaps the Angelic Forces know more than we do !

Let them choose how to give their Healing - accept that you are just a conduit for their energies, a willing tool that they use.

Ego may not like this, but Heart understands.

In cases of very severe illness with much suffering, it may not be possible (or in the Healee's best interest) for a physical healing to occur - the suffering may be mitigated by the Angelic Forces, however, until death occurs and the Soul moves on.

If you cannot obtain permission for a Healing, or the Being is far away, then you can always send them your Love and ask the Angelic Forces to send Healing Energies to them, always to be used in the 'highest and best good' of the Being.

Advanced Healing Overview

There are as many ways to help with Healing as there are stars in the sky. Not any single method is perfect - but some may be better than others in any particular circumstance.

It is important to recognize that our own method may not always work - that the method of another Healer may be more suitable for a person. We all have strengths and weaknesses - and it is when we work together in a team that more can be accomplished.

If you wish to improve your Healing abilities, you can read about the different modalities in general, select those that you think will suit you best for more study, read more in depth about these, and then work with Healers having experience in these - you will learn in practice much more than from study, but study provides a good foundation.

If you keep an open mind, you can ask 'The System' to help you to become proficient in a healing modality - you may receive hints that are not generally known, even by the experienced Teachers, and tell others so that they can improve.

A brief overview of some modalities follows.

Healing Touch, etc.

'Energy Medicine' by Donna Eden, is one of the most important Healing books. In it she uses Kinesiology, a form of Intuitive signaling. It is a magnificent explanation of meridians and points, plus Chakras and Auras, combined with the use of hands to move energies to Heal - with practical demonstrations which have been tested and work well. Videos for instruction are available.

Reiki

Reiki formulates the rituals used in Healing by using symbols. Diane Stein's book 'Essential Reiki' enables people to understand the techniques and use its Healing Power without paying enormous amounts of money for the privilege.

Rituals help you to remember the correct way to do something - a program loaded in your mind; when done by many people all over the world, the patterns are 'set in stone' - and so easily called for use by all practitioners.

Flower Essences

Particular diseases are associated with emotional problems, such as heart problems being associated with anger. The emotional problems may be alleviated by herbal essences, such as Bach Flower Remedies - but the deeper reasons for allowing hate, greed, anger, etc., to be in the person in the first place must be overcome.

It may be advantageous to use these essences to deal with the problem, and then use other methods to eliminate the causes.

Reflexology

Based on the Chinese understanding of meridians, which all have terminal or connector points at many places such as the eyes, ears, teeth, hands, and feet of a person.

The feet are excellent places to work with the meridians - they are more spaciously placed, located without undue effort, and you can work on them easily.

Reflexology practitioners can often extract 'other dimensional life forms' (such as having a pain which moves around) and give great relief; many of these take up residence (like squatters) in the meridians and the muscles of the body.

Acupuncture / Acupressure

The ancient Chinese knowledge is that there are subtle energy channels that run throughout our body, coming to the surface at certain places, and probably having connections between these places within our auric bodies.

These channels are known to surface in our feet, our hands, our ears, and our eyes. Iridology is based on examining the eyes - where indications of diseases can be recognized, even before the disease becomes apparent in the body itself.

When these channels become blocked, illness occurs; by applying pressure or lancing into the channels (especially where these channels have major points) the blockages are released, and health improved.

Shamanic Healing

This is a far deeper aspect of Healing which is beyond the scope of many. But the books 'Urban Shaman' and 'Kahuna Healing' by Serge Kahili King are well worth reading.

One simple Shamanic method is to attach all of a particular worry to a piece of paper - writing down the problem, putting all your feelings into the writing, visualizing all aspects of the problem being removed from your own Being and put into the paper; and then burning the paper.

I was with one Shaman when he cleared the 'not good' energies from a house; after working within the house, he chose a small pine tree in the garden, stripped a section of bark from around its trunk, and tied tinsel and other bright objects to the tree.

He then gave instruction to the people in the house to cut the tree down in about a week and then burn it. He explained that the tinsel and bright objects would attract 'not good' energies to the tree, and then they would be changed in form when burnt.

This may be the origin of a Christmas Tree - to clear away 'not good' energies at the end of a year, so that the New Year would start free of past negativity. Perhaps the original intent was not understood when the Christian religion included Christmas Trees as part of the Pagan Festival that they renamed Christmas !

What is the effect of hanging an effigy of an Angel on such a tree ?

One of the main ways that Shamans heal is by 'Soul Retrieval'; when a person has an intensively traumatic experience, some part of them, such as a 'Soul Piece', seems to disconnect from them.

Soul Retrieval includes identifying the trauma, locating the missing Soul Piece, persuading it that is now safe to return, assuring it that it will be welcomed and loved, and bringing it back to the rest of the Soul.

It may be that when a person dies, the chances of any missing Soul Piece being reconnected disappear; perhaps they try to have a separate existence in the 'Astral Plane'.

Perhaps other aspects of a person, that are 'not good', also separate from a Soul when it departs a human body at death. Eastern wisdom tells that these are the main inhabitants of the Astral Plane, and that they will try and get back into a living human being - usually causing unwelcome effects if successful.

For example, if such a part has been used to drug use or heavy drinking, they may hang around places where this occurs, seeking to find a human who has such a tendency, and then endeavouring to join.

Such cases are examples of the saying 'Like seeks Like'.

Of What we Think, to That we Tune
The Range being Further than the Moon

Our Intuitive Radio

We can consider ourselves as being like a radio that can transmit and receive signals, to communicate with others - including 'Upstairs'.

We are 'plugged in' because we are receiving Life energy from a well established 'mains supply' - we may not understand how this is generated, but it seems to be at the correct strength (voltage) for us.

We may even be 'switched on' - if we are open to co-operating with 'The System'; to receive help and give help to others.

There are various wave bands, and the most satisfactory is the one called Love - which is used to give support to all Beings in their endeavours to 'do what is right'.

A radio picks up all the signals (such as thoughts) that are transmitted; when we listen to a radio we choose one signal and amplify it so that it can be heard. Our own radio does this simply by thinking of who or what we wish to join in communication.

All this work is done by our Heart-Mind-Brain team - our Brain retrieves the needed frequency from its own storage, our Mind selects the station, and our Heart ensures distortion-free tuning.

If we have any sort of communication with another Being, we have stored their frequency and 'signature' (vibrational pattern) in our memory. This is also the case with any item which we have held in our hand. In some cases, when we have not had previous contact, we may have to ask, via our Heart, for the needed data.

Some people have the ability to link directly to their Heart-Mind-Brain team using their senses - or the similar senses of the Soul, as previously discussed. They are clairvoyant, feel the atmosphere, hear messages, or just 'know'.

Most of us need an earphone (or a loud-speaker) to help us hear the signals better, or a meter-like device of some description to indicate such signals.

This is the work done by our nervous-muscular system, as demonstrated in our first experiment - our body moved forward to signal YES, or backward to indicate NO.

More Body Signals

We are not restricted to just forward or back body movements - we can develop other signals. We decide on the signal, explain it to our Heart-Mind-Brain team, load it as a program, and practice with it to ensure that it is installed correctly and works properly.

Three of the very best, which I find to be extremely accurate, very fast, and not noticeable to most other people, are using Finger Tap or Slide, Eye Blinks and Tongue Signals.

Finger Tap or Slide

Use your middle finger to press down on the nail of your index finger as you ask a question - if your index finger resists a YES signal is given, collapse means NO. It is even less tiring to try to slide the middle finger from the index finger nail - YES and NO signals may vary according to which hand is used, so check !

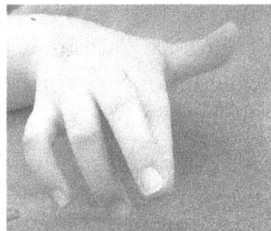

Photo from Susan Collins' book 'Bridge Matter and Spirit with Dowsing'

See www.dowser.ca

This is used by experts checking a client's health - it is fast, and does not cause any tiring, so is suitable for continual use.

Eye Blinks

One blink indicates YES, two blinks means NO, and three blinks signals that the question is not understood, or that the answer is not available.

Tongue Signals

Ask your question with your tongue midway between your upper and lower teeth, and feel where it goes - to your upper teeth for YES, or lower teeth for NO. Going to the roof or floor of your mouth indicates a very strong signal.

A variant of this is to rub your tongue over the roof of your mouth and ask your question - rough means YES, smooth NO.

Often the answer comes as I am still formulating the question in my mind ! This is wonderful when trying to work out a problem, since you are continually being guided in the right direction.

The late Dan Wilson, who was a 'leading light' in the Alternative Healing Community in England, did a brilliant job in suggesting some interesting signals. Here are his suggestions:

Basically, people are 'touchies' or 'feelies' - they naturally do Intuitive Signaling by touch or movement, or by feel or sensing.

First, what kind of question-and-answer would really be useful and interesting to you ?

This is a very personal matter, but in classes I usually suggest a few; for example:

"Is my health better than 50 per cent compared to perfect health ?"

You look for a YES or NO signal when trying 10, 20, 30, 40 etc per cent in turn; this is better than asking is it a particular percentage, since it may not be an exact number.

You HAVE to get a response somewhere so it's a good starter; 0 won't be an answer as that will require you to be dead, and if you get 100 there's probably a glitch in your system.

You can test for 'vitality' in the same way. 'Vitality' as a percentage is the proportion of your total energy available for living rather than fighting current stress factors.

'Health' is the same thing, but rolling into account all the possible stress factors you are likely to meet, being the person you are.

"What stresses me ?" Start with classes of things like food, other substance, circumstance, interrelationship, something place-linked, then hunt for detail.

"Does my car/house/TV need attention for anything ?" If YES, then ask more questions to narrow it down.

"Is my mother-in-law naturally like that, or do we wind each other up ?" A laugh in the class is never unwelcome !

When I teach people, I mix the touchy and feely systems to give everyone a chance.

<u>Whole Body</u>

Stand to attention in front of (say) the supermarket egg counter. Fix a carton of the type you are interested in with your eagle eye and ask, *"Are all these eggs fresh, good, and free from cracks ?".* A slight bow YES, a slight bending back NO.

A few people who have tried this found that they twisted round rather than bowed, and one man found that his bow was graduated, so if the eggs were very fresh indeed, he did a Japanese bow suitable for the Emperor. (I didn't ask what happened if they were totally rotten.)

Most people get a forward or backward movement. If you do not, then be alert for any other noticeable sensation, or other body part twitch or movement.

<u>Other Body Responses</u>

Many people have a hand reaction of some kind - two fingers moving apart or together, or a clenching or opening.

This energy sensation varies enormously from one person to the next, and from question to question. There are a wide variety of sensations that can be experienced, such as:

...   Tingling feelings in all of the hand or just part of the hand
...   A gentle breeze-like feeling blowing past the hand
...   A cool draft of air
...   A pressure-like pushing against an invisible barrier
...   An edge-like feeling as if an invisible sharp edge is pushing on a large or small part of your hand/fingers.
...   A gentle push on the fingertips
...   A pronounced tingling or sharp sensation in one finger only or just part of one finger only
...   A 'thud' feeling in the palm of the hand
...   A line of energy suddenly appearing across part of the hand.

Those are just a few of the common ones. Usually they are felt in the left hand, but sometimes also in the right hand, and occasionally in both hands.

Sometimes the sensation is very 'up front' and obvious, whilst at other times it is subtle. You may even get different responses for different types of questions - perhaps because the answer is coming from different sources of knowledge.

<u>Finger Thumb</u>

Think your question, or the section of it (*"is 40% correct ?"*) and rub index finger and thumb together gently.

A rough feeling indicates YES, a slippery feeling shows NO; you can have a second opinion on the finger behind, rough for NO.

This system doesn't work well for me, so I use the thumb and the next finger (my middle finger) - I get a reverse signal this way. This is similar to the Radionics 'stick pad', which you rub with a thumb to get the knob settings on the 'black boxes'.

It is very popular with Intuitive doctors who can hide their hand in their pocket for covert diagnosis and get signals about a patients health !

Two Hand Pass

A)   Place the palms of your hands together in a prayerful manner at face level.

B)   Lower the left hand to waist level.

C)   Place your awareness in the palm of your right hand, which remains in an upright position.

D)   Ask a question (which can be answered with a simple YES or NO) of your left hand.

Give yourself plenty of space and extend your left arm back as far to the left as you can. Then gradually move your left hand in the reverse direction, coming in a wide sweep at waist level towards and around your front.

Note that the left hand is kept well below the upright right hand at all times. The two hands are NEVER opposite one another at the same level.

E)   If the answer is YES, you will feel energy, or pressure, or just a strong physical inclination to stop before your left hand gets to below the right elbow. This is the energy we are talking about.

If the answer is a strong YES, the left hand will stop almost immediately, while a weak YES will be closer to the front.

If the left hand stops under the right elbow, it means 'Don't know'.

If the left hand goes cleanly past the right elbow under the right hand, then the answer is NO.

It is wise to practice this exercise over and over so you get used to the sensation in your left hand.

The easiest way to practice this is to ask YES/NO questions where you already know the answer - often the silliest and most obvious questions are the best for this practice.

Forced Blink

Consciously hold your eyes open and think your question. A blink occurring against your will signifies YES.

If you're uncertain whether a blink was a natural one or a Intuitive one, repeat the exercise using another system. After a while you can tell them apart.

I got into Intuitive Signaling via this method. I needed to find cheap fuel when driving at 70 mph, so I used the steering wheel as a 'clock face', with positions indicating numbers from 1 to 12.

Run one hand round it for direction (12 o'clock = straight ahead), then ask for mileage - first total distance, second *"How far along this road before I turn off ?"*. When you get a forced blink, you are getting the answer as shown on a clock face.

This is excellent for such things as locating radar traps, and *"When is this lady in front going to turn off ?"*

Own Aura Sensing

Find another person and see if you can 'sense their aura'. This is done simply by extending your palm towards them and expecting some kind of reaction as you enter their aura.

Sometimes this is a tingling, sometimes it's an 'invisible balloon' feeling, or just some form of gentle resistance. When you have practiced this with another person, repeat on your own self - then you know that you have an aura, and how it feels.

After that you can command your aura to be there for YES, and not be there for NO.

Bingo - you have a Intuitive Signaling system up and running.

A variation of this is to hold your hands apart, palms open and facing each other; now move your palms together slowly, and you will feel auric energy - just some form of gentle resistance.

You can command this auric energy to be there for YES, and be absent for NO. Very simple and effective !

Hand Jab

Ask your question and thrust your right or left hand down sharply as though trapping a bouncing tennis ball. The hand closing spontaneously means NO, opening out YES.

Because of its dynamic movement, this system is excellent for forcing weak Intuitive Signaling to become stronger - 'bursting the paper wall of fear'.

The jab can be upwards, as in a class I gave to the Surrey Dowsers in Surbiton (a suburb of London).

As soon as I suggested the method, about fifty ladies were leaping about the room, jabbing into the air and laughing fit to bust. They were checking on their neighbours, the naughty girls.

As one said, *"If her fancy man parks his Mercedes round the block and I can check what he's doing in there, it's only like having another pair of eyes, isn't it ?"*

I don't know if this preoccupation is shared in other great cities !

Slinky

A 'slinky' is one of those machined spiral metal coils which if you place one at the top of a staircase and push it over, it will somersault slowly down the stairs.

Imagine you are holding one upright in your right palm, place your left palm next to it but lower, like a stair, and ask your question.

If you feel the 'slinky' arriving in your left palm (and/or your hands rising/ lowering to match the change in weight) that signifies YES - no change signals NO.

For me this works purely by hand movement - I can't feel the slinky. A variant of this movement is:

Wrist Twist

Hold your hand-shaking hand out as though about to shake hands with someone invisible, thumb upwards, then think your question. Your hand usually twists clockwise for YES, or counter/anti-clockwise for NO.

Chain Link

Gently pinch your right thumb and first finger together, enclose them in a similar left-handed pinch (as if they were two links in a chain), ask your question, and then try to pull apart. Success signifies YES, failure NO.

Opposed Thumbs

Place your hands (palms open towards your body) in front of you as though sheltering your stomach, with the eight fingers hanging down almost parallel and the two thumbs upwards, pressing hard against one another in an upside-down V.

Ask your question and the two thumbs flick away from you for YES and towards you for NO. In my case, I find I can get rough numbers up to 10 immediately, because the thumb movements are graduated over a 90 degree range.

The significance can be reversed for some individuals, or by willpower, or against your will when you get tired (this is sometimes called 'switching').

You have to find out which is which by asking establishing questions to which you know the answer, or command *"Show me my YES signal !"*

Point-&-Sense

Ask your question and point at the possible answers, which you have attributed mentally to the fingers of the non-pointing hand. A distinctive sensation (a sting in the neck or ear lobe is common) signifies YES.

Invisible Balloon

Use one hand to sense with and the other (or the wall) as a wall. Ask your question and move this hand towards the 'wall'.

An invisible balloon (or prickly ball, or cold area, etc.) getting in the way signifies YES - bigger and harder, a surer one.

You can play around with this a lot - e.g. have balloons signifying NO, or have different areas on the wall for diagnostic balloons giving you choices, numbers, times, etc. The 'balloon' is used a lot to sense auras and energy bodies.

Finger Wiggle

Hold your hands limp and ask your question. If the fingers of one hand flutter like a curtain in a breeze the signal is YES; if the fingers of the other hand flutter, NO. Check which hand gives which signal !

Nod

Hold head straight as weakly as will just keep it from flopping, and ask your question. An involuntary nod indicates YES; NO might be signaled by a shake sideways or a jerk backwards.

Robot Nose

Similar to Nod - but using your field of view and blinks.

Keep your eyes looking ahead and ask your question, which then will be answered by something in your field of view (*"Which melon tastes best ?"*)

Allow your nose to point to the answer. Another method is to move your eyes across the scene from left to right, imagining a vertical cursor line. An involuntary blink means: the sought goodie is on this line.

Then hold your eyes on the line and scan up and down. A blink means that you are looking at it. This is especially good when picking stones or shells off a beach.

You can keep a reserve blink for something which is hidden underneath the top layer(s) - very good in supermarkets where the best fruit or vegetable is some way down in the pile. Rummage on the chosen coordinates until you get a blink.

Finger Lift

Rest a wrist on your chest or a chair arm so that the fingers are free to move but extended. Ask one finger to rise to signal YES. When one rises, ask for another to signal NO.

You can even assign other fingers for other responses.

Be sure that you're not moving the fingers voluntarily. If you prefer, you can choose which fingers signal which responses, e.g. use only one hand. You may notice a tingling or other sensation.

In a watchful state this method may require time and some effort. Under hypnosis it's rare for it not to work.

Finger Tap

Use your middle finger to press down on the nail of your index finger as you ask a question - if your index finger resists a YES signal is given, collapse means NO.

This is used by experts checking a client's health - it is fast, and does not cause any tiring, so is suitable for continual use.

Dan Wilson's Comments

In all these cases, the significance can be reversed for some individuals, or by willpower, or against your will when you get tired; this is called 'switching'.

You have to find out which is which by asking establishing questions to determine your YES signal.

If you do not get any response, it may mean *"That was not the right question to ask !"*, that the question was not understood, or that an answer was not available.

If you get greatly exaggerated responses, you may be getting 'YES stronger than YES' - also called 'yes-beyond-yes', and a similar extra-strong NO.

These signify answers which are more positive or negative than you have allowed for in your question.

> *"Has my daughter passed her exam ?"*
>> Yes-beyond-yes 'she came top'.
> *"Will my plane leave on time ?"*
>> No-beyond-no 'Flight Cancelled'.

In Healing, Intuitive Signaling can be used to find ways of remedying tensions quickly - identifying the causes, and asking about solutions.

I Wonder, Wonder, Wonder When,
And then I Wonder More Again.

Amplifying Intuitive Signals

It is most important to remember that Intuitive signals are originated by our Heart-Mind-Brain team (our Heart being our Intuitive link to 'Upstairs', working closely with the Intuitive part of our Mind-Brain) and then manifested by our nervous-muscular system to give physical movements in our bodies.

We have discussed the use of our sense of balance, and used it in our first experiment; we have balance sensors throughout our bodies, and the signals given by our sense of balance can be amplified.

Let us experiment with using our hands to indicate YES or NO. Get a mug, and put some water in it, almost full - so that you can see any movement due to tilting, but not spill the water.

Hold the mug in one of your hands so it is level (elbows loosely at you side, arm then extended at about waist level); now stop looking at the mug (to look straight ahead is best) and formulate a simple YES/NO question (to start, know the true answer) in the logical part of your mind.

Now ask your Heart this question, and say (silently, to yourself) *"I wonder ..., I wonder ..., I wonder ...,"* and then look to see what has happened to the water in the mug.

Saying *"I wonder ..., I wonder ..., I wonder ...,"* keeps the logical part of your mind very busy - wondering what it is wondering about, so that it does not interfere with the rest of your Heart-Mind-Brain team.

You will probably find that the water in the mug shows that the mug has tilted towards the centre-front of your body for YES (if holding the mug in your right hand, the water is in the left part of the mug), and in the opposite direction for a NO.

A simple explanation of this would be that if you asked *"Do I like ice-cream ?"* (or your favourite food or drink) and had held mugs in both hands, then they would tilt towards each other to signal a 'joining' for YES, or a 'dispersion' for NO.

There are probably a few problems that would arise if you carried almost full mugs of water around with you whenever you might need to get an Intuitive answer to a question ! How can this be overcome ?

The signal that you are receiving is being made by the slight twisting of your arm, wrist, and hand muscles. It is this movement that we need to amplify, so that we can get good and clear signals.

You could hold a straw or a stick in each hand, and see if they move in- or out-wards; there are other ways, however, that have been used for centuries - and proven to work well.

Intuition on Building Sites

You will find many plumbers, electrical workers, and water-works employees who use a piece of bent wire - it is cheap, does not break, is easy to carry, simple to use, and proven to be effective.

They use it to locate water pipes and buried wires - they have success even when the original engineering drawings were incorrect or have been lost. Beyond just locating the pipe or wire, they can even locate the spot where there is a leak or break.

This 'Pipe Locator' is usually a length of strong wire (perhaps a welding rod) bent in a 'L' shape - the shorter length being the handle, and the longer length the pointer.

It needs to be held correctly; the operator's elbow should be loose at his side, with the forearm, wrist, and hand extended forward.

The handle should hold the handle strongly enough to give good support, but loosely enough so that the pointer can swing easily.

To start, the pointer is guided to be pointing forwards; this means that it is hanging down slightly, so that gravity keeps it forward - but not hanging down so far that it will not sway when the operator's wrist and hand give a slight twist.

The operator tunes his Heart-Mind-Brain 'radio', concentrating his thoughts to whatever is being sought, such as picturing a pipe - or water leaking from a pipe.

Now he walks slowly forward, and the pointer may swing (usually in, towards his body centre) to indicate that his Heart-Mind-Brain team has found resonance between the tuned thought and what is being sought; then the operator marks this point on the ground in some way.

It is important to have a clear and precise understanding in your Mind as to the exact point that is indicated - the end of the rod, your hand, or where your toes are located.

It is customary to then approach this point from the opposite side, and locate a similar point of first contact. The item being sought can generally be found half way between these two points of first contact. The depth often equals the distance from either first point of contact to the centre.

This whole procedure may be repeated at other places nearby, to confirm the location of the pipe or wire.

If a leak or break is sought, the operator will then follow along the indicated location of the pipe or wire, picturing the leak or break in his Mind, and using his wire (sometimes called an 'L' rod) as before to find where it is.

Making your own 'L' Rod

If you do not have an 'L' rod, get hold of a metal coat hanger, cut off the hook section, and cut the bottom bar in the centre; you now have two pieces of wire - bend them so that they form a right angle at the bend, and you now have two 'L' rods.

If you wish, you can cut a drinking straw in two, and slip each half over a handle of your 'L' rods. Keep the uncut edge uppermost - if the cut edge rubs against the pointer it may catch and stop free rotation.

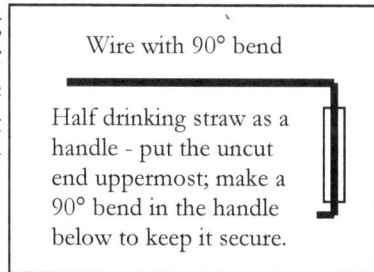

Wire with 90° bend

Half drinking straw as a handle - put the uncut end uppermost; make a 90° bend in the handle below to keep it secure.

Signals Used

The basic signals for use with an 'L' rod are 'joining is positive, separation is negative'. The amount of movement, the degree of change, indicates the strength of the signal.

If we imagine our 'L' rod to be the hour hand of a clock, with the 12 o'clock mark furthest from us, then movement between the 11 and 1 marks indicates searching - trying to get the answer, and not the answer itself.

With your 'L' rod held in your right [left] hand, 10 [2] indicates a weak YES, with the strength rising to a strong YES at 8 [4].

If it goes to 7 [5] this is a 'YES-beyond-YES', a better than expected result. The signals for NO are reversed: 2 - 4 [10 - 8], with 'NO-beyond-NO' at 5 [7].

Many people use an 'L' rod in each hand; the advantage is that you get confirmation when they both give the same answer.

Should they differ, check your question, or stand up and ask your Heart the same question and see whether you move forwards or backwards.

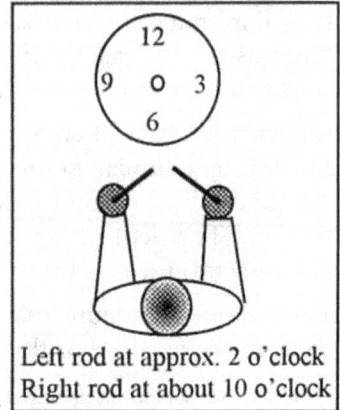

Left rod at approx. 2 o'clock
Right rod at about 10 o'clock

In all such cases, be aware of the very first thought that 'pops' into your Mind - this comes from your Intuition, and will probably assist you to correct any problem with your question.

There is little training needed with 'L' rods - just hold in your Mind the clock face and meanings attached, and practice - seek where the water supply comes into you home from the street, or see if you can locate any underground streams in your area.

Pointing with your 'L' Rods

You can ask that your 'L' rod points to something that you seek - hold a picture of it in your Mind, or even a sample like it (or belonging to it) in one of your hands. Then hold your 'L' rod in the search position, and slowly rotate yourself, preferably in a clockwise direction.

You may find that the pointer of your 'L' rod stops moving with you, holding in one direction. You can follow the line indicated - or just note where it points, then go to another place, repeat the search, and note where the line now indicated cross the first line, and go there.

One peculiar aspect of this is tracking - your 'L' rod may lead you along taken by the item sought, not directly to its present location.

This can be useful in tracking the route taken by a criminal, to find clues left along the way, but it can confuse a person who does not understand what is happening.

Frank was attending a meeting; when they left, a fellow attendee realized that his wallet had been stolen. Frank took his 'L' rod, and followed the track; it led to an open trench in the road where new sewage pipes were being installed.

The general consensus was *"A waste of time, that sort of thing does not work"*. Frank, however, had faith ! He leant over the side of the trench, and saw the wallet stuck in the trench supports - where it had been thrown by the thief.

On one occasion a very experienced operator was demonstrating pointing to a good sized audience, and asked *"Please point to North"*. Everybody knew that the building was built North-South, but his 'L' rod kept pointing at an angle !

Finally a man in the audience stood up, and said *"It is pointing at me - my name is Tom North !"*

Is the Baby a Boy ?

There are many stories of ladies holding a needle and thread over a future mother's stomach and asking this question - and they are surprisingly correct most of the time !

If there is an error, it is usually in the question asked - *"Is it a boy or a girl ?"* will give a YES signal, because it could be either.

Sometimes a pendant, crystal on a chain, a cross, or other type of Pendulum is used. The item used is not important - it is just a tool being used by the Heart-Mind-Brain team via the nervous-muscular system, again using the balance receptors to cause movements of the forearm, wrist, and hand.

The manipulation of these is far more complicated than with an 'L' rod, but the principle remains the same.

The signals used may vary; this does not matter, so long as they are understood by the operator. The operator may even decide to change the signals or their meaning - and this works, so long as the sub-conscious Mind understands the new system.

This method is also used in many egg hatcheries to determine the sex of the unborn chicks - with great success even on a commercial basis.

The signals are usually based on the subject or answer being Positive/YES or Negative/NO.

This Positive/Negative is like comparing the direction of a flow - from the positive to the negative.

Male is generally seen by the Heart-Mind-Brain team as being positive, giving out energy. Female is seen as negative in the sense of being receptive.

Thus the best way of forming the sex question is to ask *"Is the unborn male ?"* since a YES signal is also appropriate for Positive-Male. Of course, it also pays to check if twins can be expected, and if so, to ask additional questions.

Making and Holding your Pendulum

You can make your Pendulum by having any form of weight suspended by a flexible connector that you can hold in your hand. You can tie a piece of string around a metal nut, for example.

You can also use a crystal on a chain, a cross or other neck decoration, or a glass bead on a length of cord. Some people use specially shaped Pendulums - because energies are very responsive to shapes, to forms of structure.

But even so, the main movement originates from your Heart-Mind-Brain team via your nervous-muscular system - YOU are the most important part !

You will find it best to hold your Pendulum with the string, cord, or chain between your thumb and first finger.

A long length of string enables you to see the movement more easily, but the speed of movement is slow.

A very short length moves very fast, but the amount of movement is less, making it more difficult to see - a real problem when you are starting !

Probably the best length to use when starting is about six inches (15 cm) - then as you get more experienced, you can reduce this to between 3 and 4 inches (7 and 10 cm), as you find suits you.

Some LOLs (Little Old Ladies) are absolute wizards at using a Pendulum; their friends may watch them, and try to do the same: *"It doesn't work for me !"* they cry. Why is this so ?

In most cases this is because they have not trained their system to give signals.

This is like telling a five year old child *"Give me the first five numbers in the Fibonacci series"* - he does not have any idea of what is meant, which of his toys you want.

Now it may work if you ask your Heart *"Please give me a signal with my Pendulum that indicates YES"* and then watch to see if your Pendulum moves. Repeat the question for NO, and for NOT AVAILABLE, and remember the signals. Then you can ask questions.

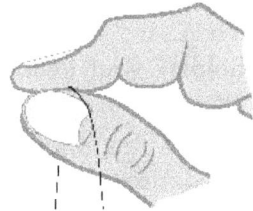

Signals used with your Pendulum

A Pendulum is able to move in more directions than an 'L' rod, so the signaling can be more extensive - swinging to and fro in various directions, or rotating clockwise or anti-clockwise, or even making elliptical combinations of these movements.

Again, the strength of the movement indicates the strength of the answer.

Basically, there are two major systems of signaling - perhaps described as being Physical or Meta-Physical.

The Physical system is similar to that used by 'L' rods - to and fro indicates a joining (the food is good for you to eat), side to side a separation (a barrier between the food and yourself - do not eat it, for whatever reason).

The Meta-Physical system is rotational - YES, positive, male, inputting an energy, and sending Love being clockwise; NO, negative, female, extracting an energy being anti-clockwise. Note that there is no 'taking of Love' !

It may be best to decide which signal you want to use, and then train your Heart-Mind-Brain team and your nervous-muscular system to give these. I find the following best:

WAITING	To and fro swing
YES	Clockwise circle
NO	Anticlockwise circle
NOT AVAILABLE	Side to side swing

So for each of these signals, make your Pendulum give the signal by using all your muscles in your forearm, wrist, and hand - exaggerating these movements (since you are in a training session).

Then say *"This is a [to and fro swing], it signals [WAITING]!"* , and then holding your Pendulum still, and asking *"Please give me the signal for [WAITING]"*.

Repeat this until you get a good response for the signal being installed, and then do the same training session for the next signal, until they are all satisfactory.

It is best to do these in the order shown, since you can go into the WAITING mode before getting the other signals - it is easier for your Pendulum to change its movement rather than start from being still.

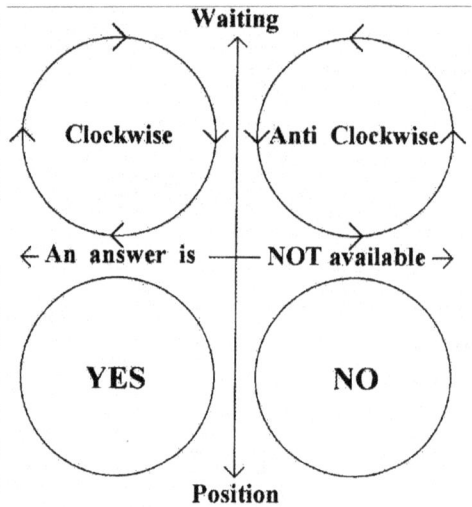

Waiting

Clockwise   **Anti Clockwise**

← **An answer is** ──── **NOT available** →

YES   **NO**

Position

Pointing - with your Pendulum

One of the very good reasons for using a circle to signal YES or NO is that when you seek by asking your Pendulum to point towards something, you can check that it is giving a good signal.

Install a program to define the signals used by your Pendulum: *"When my Pendulum points to an item, it will first give a YES signal to indicate that it is the correct direction, or a NO signal to show that a problem exists"*.

A linear signal for YES or NO could be confused with the direction sought - the circular signals avoid this problem.

Remember that your Pendulum swings in two directions - so if you are lost and seeking the direction to your home, or locating an item that you have lost, see the way that your Pendulum swings (to north-south, east-west, etc.), then point to one of them (north or south, etc.) with your hand and ask *"Is this the correct direction ?"*

Simple Counting

A simple way of getting experience with pointing is to practice with this 'Counting Chart':

1. Hold your Pendulum over the 'Start Here'.
2. Ask your Pendulum to point to a number that you choose.
3. Check that your Pendulum makes a clockwise circle - to indicate 'OK'.
4. Check that it does point along the line of the number chosen.
5. Repeat with other numbers.

See where your Pendulum points when you choose a fractional number: like 3¼.

Pointing is a most useful way of using your Pendulum - so the amount of time that you spend on practice is not wasted.

Pendulum Dowsing

9   0
8
7
6
5
4
3
2
1   0

Start Here

Counting Chart

It is time well spent - some examples follow.

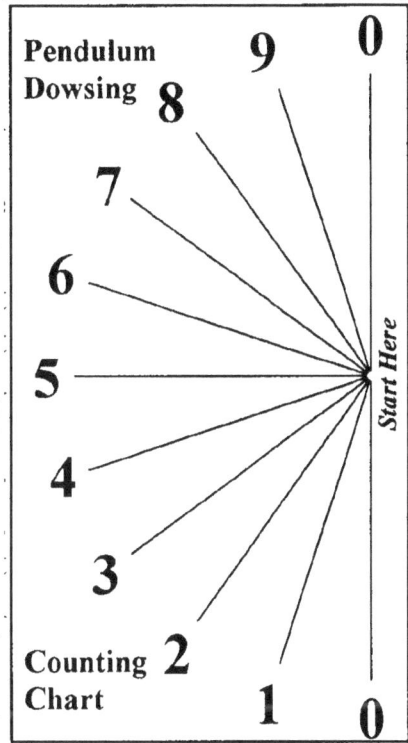

Segment Selection

One of the benefits of pointing with your Pendulum is that you can make a segmented diagram, each segment identified with an option - such as writing the names of various places to go on holiday in each segment.

Then ask *"Which is the [best place for me to go on my next holiday] ?"* and see which is indicated by your Pendulum.

It is also best to label one segment as 'Other' - and if that segment is indicated, listen for the first thought that 'pops' into your Mind.

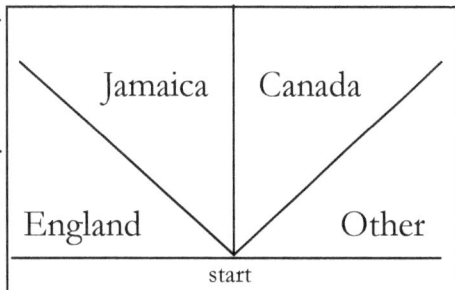

Jamaica   Canada

England   Other

start

Selection from Lists

You can use your Pendulum to select an item in a list, even to identify problems in a computer program. You can do this by holding it to one side and see where it points, or use your other hand to point with a pencil or your finger to items until your Pendulum gives a YES signal.

When you get one selection, ask if there is also another to be found - you may have more than one error in a program, or need more than one supplement if you are checking what is needed for your good health.

Your Handy Chart

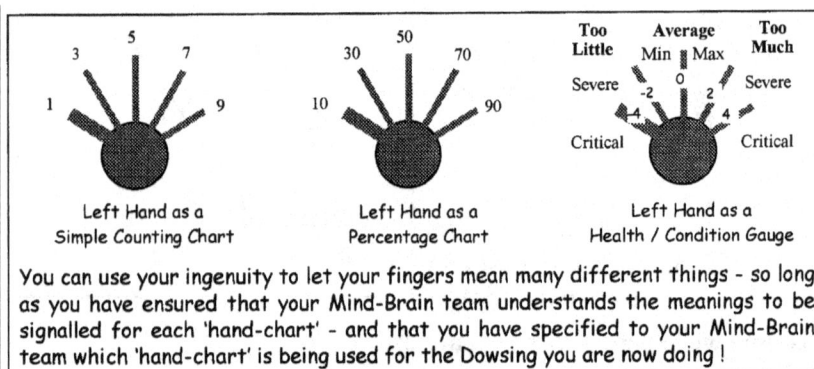

Left Hand as a Simple Counting Chart	Left Hand as a Percentage Chart	Left Hand as a Health / Condition Gauge

You can use your ingenuity to let your fingers mean many different things - so long as you have ensured that your Mind-Brain team understands the meanings to be signalled for each 'hand-chart' - and that you have specified to your Mind-Brain team which 'hand-chart' is being used for the Dowsing you are now doing !

Since most of us have two hands, we can use the spare one (the one not holding your Pendulum !) as a chart for many purposes.

It is best to use signals that conform to indicators that you see often, such as the speedometer and charging gauge of your car - your mind-brain team is accustomed to the signals used.

This is a quick way to check on your health or vitality, if medications are beneficial to you, how many tablets should be taken (dose, doses per day - these may change with effect already achieved), percentage accuracy of a statement, etc.

Historical Background

Feng Shui is based on Dowsing used in China 4,000 years ago.

This method of working with your Intuition is generally called 'Radiesthesia', 'Dowsing', or sometimes when locating wells 'Water Witching'.

The interesting point about this terminology is that the Roman Catholic priests used these methods themselves, but if any person who was not ordained used them, they were described as using 'witchcraft'.

The Spanish priests used this a lot when they invaded the Americas - and the hint of witchcraft was quite effective in preventing others from competing to find hoards of gold.

One way of dealing with people believed to be dabbling in witchcraft was to use a 'ducking stool' - they were tied to this on the end of a long plank, and doused into water until they repented.

If they repented whilst under water, it was difficult to hear them - so many drowned. The term 'Dowsing' may have originated due to this practice.

Current Attitudes

One's personal attitude should be based on sincerity - as when in prayer.   Sometimes the action requested by prayer does not materialize - and people wonder *"why ?"*.

Most often the reply comes through one's Intuition - not the logical part of our mind-brain team. The more open that we are to our Intuition, the more likely that we will be aware of any response to our prayer - perhaps further action is needed from us before 'Upstairs' can give the requested help.

Dealing with Spiritual matters has long been considered the domain of religious organizations; indeed it is helpful if people are guided onto the 'good' path.

But the aim of helping has often become converted into the target of control. 'Our way is the only way !' - or else you are damned.

Most ministers of religion believe in what they are doing, and genuinely want to help others - they deserve our respect and gratitude, especially those who are in daily touch with those that are suffering, and give them assistance.

The problem may be within the bureaucracy of the religious organization - the corporate mentality 'We are better than the rest - and are going to be bigger'.

Sometimes the number of 'Souls' in their 'bag' matters more than the quality of life - Spiritual or otherwise.

In past centuries people were discouraged from reading in case they could learn from the Bible - and services were spoken in Latin, not understood by most of the congregations.

Many organizations are being downsized, and the cut happens most often to the middle management - those between the top guys upstairs, and those below who make things happen. The people in the middle do not like this change, and will do their best to prevent it.

Perhaps the bureaucracies of the religious organizations can be considered to be like the middle management - getting between 'Upstairs' and the people.

When they think that a person is by-passing them and going directly to 'Upstairs', many of them feel threatened (it must be the work of the devil !) instead of understanding that their correct purpose has been achieved.

"Is She Pretty or Ugly ?"

- "Pretty Ugly !"

Asking Questions

This sounds very simple - everyone knows how to ask a question - we do it every day.

But it is actually the cause of many misunderstandings - you know what you mean to ask, but the respondent mistakes your meaning, gives you the answer to a slightly different question.

You may even misunderstand this reply - especially if the answer given was not complete, but presumed that you knew some aspect, but this was not so.

In some cases the words used may be ignored, because the listener concentrates more on the tone used than the words spoken !

Problems also may arise when a person strong in one sense (seeing, hearing, feeling, or knowing) converses with others whose prime senses differ.

When you are working with your own Intuition some of these problems may not be relevant, but it is still best to be aware that they could exist - and do your best to avoid them.

Asking Your Intuition

It is important that whenever you work with your Intuitive team (your Heart-Mind-Brain team) you are being sincere - never being frivolous. Questions that you ask for training purposes are not frivolous, since you are being sincere in improving your abilities.

Sincere means being in a similar state of Mind to prayer, since you are working with the same Beings 'Upstairs' - but you do not have to be on bended knee, shut your eyes, or hold your hands in front of you.

A good way to start is to open by asking the help and protection of 'Upstairs': *"I open in True Holy Love and Love of Truth; I ask the Force for Good to help my Intuitive team, and to ensure that all the answers given are the truth as best as I can understand, obtained from all sources that are 'In the Light'. I send you my gratitude, thanks, and Love for the help that you give."*

It is very worthwhile to then check that you have a 'green light' - so ask *"Is my Intuitive team now ready, willing, and able to so work with the 'Force for Good' ?"* or a similar question.

The questions that you ask must be absolutely clear in your mind, and be in simple language such as a child would understand.

The clarity must include avoiding any words having a double meanings, or express which alternative is meant.

I was speaking on the telephone to a clairvoyant friend, and told her that I had lost my glasses. She replied "Look by the sink in the kitchen". She was correct, but I had meant my spectacles, and she was locating glass tumblers.

Some Important Rules

There are some very important rules about the questions that you ask. While your Intuitive team may be able to understand your intention, it may still insist that you 'cover all your bases' to get you into a good habit.

And this habit is important, since at times you may address questions to an animal, a tree, your car or your computer; they will respond to the exact question that you ask - even if it is not what you intended !

First, you should be in a state of meditation or prayer - be serious, concentrate.

Second, the question must be clear, so that your Intuitive team really understands the question.

If you are thinking about eating more ice cream the question *"Is it OK ?"* is NOT clear - your Intuitive team may not understand what you mean by 'it' ! So ask *"Is it OK for me to eat more ice cream now ?"* - including to state 'when' !

Imagine that you are in a car which has a broken fuel gauge; you ask *"Does the car need gas ?"* The answer will always be YES, even if the tank is full. The car needs gasoline (called 'gas') to make the engine work, and it needs air (another gas) to burn with the gasoline and to fill the tyres. A better way to ask this question would be *"Is the fuel tank of this car less than half full ?"*.

Third, the answer must be YES or NO (if not a direction). If somebody told you a story, asking *"Is the story true ?"* may not work, because some of it may be true, and some of it may not be true.

So you must ask about the part of the story that you think may be untrue.

<u>Fourth,</u> there are some questions which should NOT be asked - especially if the question is NOT your business ! This is why it is very important to ask for permission before asking the actual question, if it may be in this category.

Included in this category are any questions concerning the time of future death of any person, including yourself.

<u>Fifth,</u> you must check that you are working within the 'rules of the game'. This means that you must define your question and the reason for asking it, and check with your Intuitive tool for YES answers to "*Can I ? May I ? Should I ?*".

This is most important if you are working on another person - but you can always just send them True Holy Love, to be used in the way that is for their Highest and Best Good without checking.

...   "*I am seeking to find the best way to ....*" to define the problem.

...   "*This is to help XXX to feel happier*" to explain your reason for asking.

...   "*Can I ask ?*" to inquire if you have the skill and knowledge to get a correct answer.

...   "*May I ask ?*" to get permission to proceed, and confirm that the answer is available.

...   "*Should I ask ?*" in case your question is about a forbidden subject, an invasion of a person's privacy, or other reason why you should not ask at this time.

If any reply is NO, you do NOT proceed; if you are asking about someone else, and did not explain that you are asking in order to help, you may get a NO answer; this is one time when you can explain why you are asking, and repeat your check. It may just be the wrong time to ask the question, or to take action.

Some people try and combine these, by presuming that getting a YES after asking "*Can I ?*" implies that permission would only be granted if the "*May I ?*" and "*Should I ?*" were also YES.

This is logical; but your intuition is NOT logical ! It is best to ask ALL the questions separately, or ask them all together!

If you get wrong answers after your "*Can I ? May I ? Should I ?*" requests, check why; it is probably due to badly worded questions, or to your influence in wanting a particular answer.

Make sure that your questions are clear and cannot be twisted (like the gas example), ask your question if the replies have all been YES, and then having asked the question say to yourself *"I wonder . . . I wonder . . . I wonder . . . "* to keep your egoistic logical mind busy wondering about wondering and avoid its interference.

Sixth, concentrate on what you are asking. Asking about something you do not like (broccoli ?) and then thinking of an ice cream will be sure to give you a wrong answer !

You must not try to make your Intuitive tool move in any way. If you try to force it to move YES because you want it to, but think that the true answer may be NO, then you are spoiling the training that you have done. So the next time you ask a question, your Intuitive team may not give the correct answer.

It is good practice to always check the answers that you get by asking *"Is the answer ... YYYY ... correct ?"* - it may be wrong if the question was poorly worded or should not have been asked.

"Is my understanding that (the answer you perceived) correct ?" is a good way to check that you have understood what was told !

Practice

Remember how to ask a question; although it may seem silly to ask permission for very simple questions, do it to build a routine to use when asking more complicated questions - 'get into the habit'.

"May I ask if my eyes are brown ?" then *"Are my eyes brown ?"*, and afterwards check by *"Is the answer that my eyes are brown correct ?"*

Ask questions such as:
...   *"Are my eyes brown ?"*,
...   *"Did I eat an egg for breakfast today ?"*
...   *"Do I like spinach ?"   Ice Cream ? Broccoli ?*
...   *"Will I be rich ?   poor ?"*

Did you ask the *"Can I? May I? Should I ?"* questions ? - and did you check the answers ?   Did you remember to 'open' correctly?

If YES to both rich and poor, remember you could be poor at one time and rich in another. Are you poor in spirit and rich in wealth ? Try asking about wealth, and about spirit !

When asking about the future, understand that the answer will be given in terms of the likely outcome of the situations and conditions that now exist - these may be changed, by yourself and by others who are involved.

If you try to influence your Intuitive tool it could give you the answer that you want - and one that may not be true ! Try and keep an open and inquiring mind, and always check the answer - ask *"Have I correctly understood the Truth ?"* or *"What is the percentage of the Truth that I have understood ?"*.

Some Hints

You do not have to speak aloud when you ask your Intuitive team a question - it is quite OK to 'think' the question to yourself. And that way, nobody else knows the question that you are asking !

The size of the swing that your Pendulum makes, such as a small circle (or a small swing), or does this slowly, is indicating that there is some doubt, or the question may be poorly worded. A very large circle (with speed) means 'without any doubt'; usually you get a middle sized circle, meaning that the answer is based on present data which may change in the future.

Remember that the size and speed is relative to the normal size and speed of a circle made with that same length of string.

Another time when you may get a small circle is when your solution to a problem is workable, but not the best solution - so keep refining your solution and you will get a bigger circle the closer that you come to the best solution.

Although your Intuitive team is able to answer all your questions, you must not rely on it for every minor matter in your daily life !

You must learn to make your own decisions; but it is OK to ask for training purposes, and if the matter is important.

And even then, it is best to make a decision and then ask *"Did I make the correct decision ?"*. If the answer is NO (or a weak YES) then work with your Intuitive team to find out how you can improve your decision.

Using your Intuition about other people is fine, providing that you stay within 'the rules'.

You can always ask how you will get on with a person. *"Can I trust Pat ?"*, *"Is Pat telling me the truth ?"*, *"Will Pat be a good friend to me ?"* and *"Has Pat taken my pencil ?"* are all excellent questions to ask.

But it is wrong to ask these same questions when they concern Pat and some other person - you should only ask if YOU are involved.

Asking about some one else, such as *"Has Pat any allergies ?"* is wrong unless Pat has given permission for the question to be asked. This is like poking your nose into another person's diary !

But if you are preparing a meal which Pat may eat and 'need to know' then explain the situation, ask permission, and you will probably be granted permission and given the required answer.

This 'need to know' is also applicable to Healing - there are a few times when Healing is 'not permitted'; if you run into such a case, you can ask if you can be told the reason.

Asking *"Is my girl/boy friend interested in another person ?"* will always tell you YES - but the sort of interest may not be what you meant !

The 'another person' may be you, the interest may be for business reasons, or because they are relatives - or they may be a fan of a film star. We are all interested in many other people.

Multiple and Imprecise Questions

Quite often we ask multiple questions in one sentence when speaking to some one else - hopefully they will give separate answers to each question.

When seeking YES/NO answers, this does not work !

Also, the English language is excellent for its imprecision - meanings being reversed according to the sense used !

A few examples, some with bar room connotations:

"Will the baby be a boy or a girl ?"
> YES - unless it is a puppy ! Twins ?

"Do you want bread or a roll for your breakfast ?"
> A roll in bed with Honey may be preferred.

"Is she pretty or ugly ?"
> *"Yes - pretty ugly !"*

"Does this road go to [London] ?" - *"Yes"*
> But it may be the long way or the worst road.

"Do you have the time ?" - *"Yes"* (but not tell it !)
     Or *"Yes, but not the inclination !"*
"Does your dog bite ?" - *"No"* - CLOMP !
     "That is not MY dog". (Peter Sellers)
"Follow me, men - I'm right behind you !"
     A certain General Officer talks.

Greater Depth Needed

"Should I marry Pat ?"

To learn forgiveness, or some other lesson ? Best to define what you are looking for: long, happy marriage based on mutual respect and love.

"Will Pat be a good employee ?"

Good for whom ? Specify honesty, loyalty to firm, punctuality, lack of absenteeism, get on well with other staff and customers.

"Will this house suit me ?"

Will it also suit the rest of your family (except mother-in-law) ? Check also about structural strength, possible gas or water leaks.

"Should I buy this car for my wife ?"

Depends - it may be a wonderful car for her, or save the trouble of a divorce (remember the man whose wife wanted a Jaguar - he bought her one, and it ate her ?).

"Will this car last a long time ?"

Yes - but not move. Check if any problems within next 5 years for tyres, steering, engine, transmission, etc.; and if you will enjoy trouble-free and safe motoring in it.

"Will I win the lottery ?"

Which lottery ? Perhaps a $5 win next year ! This is a win ! Define how much, and when - and remember that because you want to win so much, you may be influencing the answer.

In all these cases, it may be best to ask each sub-query as a separate question - then you may be guided as to further questions to ask, and will be aware of reasons which may be pertinent in making your decision.

The more important the decision, the more time and care is best invested in thinking about possible problems - and the questions to be asked to properly identify them.

For example, imagine that you are thinking of buying a house; if you have identified possible problems then you can ask about them - and perhaps drive a better bargain.

In the same vein, you can ask *"What is the minimum amount that the vendor will accept ?"* and *"How much should I offer ?"* - and use your Intuitive counting methods to get answers.

Practice makes perfect - so now spend a few minutes forming and writing down questions that are pertinent to you, and write down the answers - writing down impresses the gist into your memory, and you can learn a lot from looking at these at a later date.

Wishful Thinking Leads to Naught,
Effort is Needed for What is Sought.

The Power of Thought

Human Beings are creators. As are beavers, viruses, ants, bees and their kind, birds, moles, rabbits, and a few more species. Most other than Humans just create their own nests or homes.

Man seems different in that we create things that affect most other life forms - not in just repeating what has been made before, but new forms and devices.

Humans do not yet have the ability to create life, but to manipulate matter and other life forms for their own purposes - not all results being beneficial to humans or others.

We are, in many respects, just like the student apprentice to a magician, as portrayed in Tchaikovsky's 'Sorcerer's Apprentice', who has some skills, does not understand the consequences of mis-using them, and creates chaos.

Mystics tell that all our thoughts go into the 'cosmic collection' or similar label, similar to Rupert Sheldrake's 'Metamorphic Field' - where they remain for ever. Both the good and the bad !

If one life form develops a new skill, and this is copied by others and found to be useful, it then quickly spreads to others - even those who are not in physical contact with the originators.

There are many examples of this, such as the 'Hundredth Monkey' when one monkey washed its food, others living on the same island copied this practice and found it to be good, and suddenly it spread to monkeys on other islands.

Another occurred in Europe; glass milk bottles had metal foil caps, and were placed by the milkmen on the doorsteps of customers. A 'Blue Tit' (name of a particular bird in England) discovered that it could peck through the foil and enjoy drinking the cream - and suddenly this practice spread throughout Europe.

Scientists have had a number of occasions when they made new compounds, expecting to get a particular result - but this did not happen.

Yet when many more scientists did the same work, the expected results started to happen - and were repeated in all further experiments.

Thoughts are Broadcast

When we have a thought, get a feeling, or express an emotion, we broadcast it to 'All that Is', as do all animals, reptiles, insects, and plants. Perhaps the unimportant broadcasts are dissipated over time, but those that 'The System' considers to be noteworthy seem to be stored - added to 'The System's' store of knowledge or retained as memories in any stones or crystals affected.

A thought that is broadcast is like a pebble thrown into a pond - it sends ripples that travel the whole surface, perhaps meeting other ripples and changing to jointly form an interference pattern, similar to that used in a holograph.

We, and 'All that Is', receive these complicated interference patterns; from our interpretation of these interference patterns we formulate our own actions.

Thus each thought that we have (and broadcast) has a potential effect in the future, both our future and that of others.

Our thoughts are broadcast as a symbols - which seem to be universal, understood by animal and plant life, and by Beings 'Upstairs'. Are the crop circles that appear in fields these symbols ? Although our conscious selves may not have direct understanding of these symbols, they may be recognized by our sub-consciousness.

Our Own Thoughts

On a personal basis, when we have good or bad thoughts about another person, the effect can be observed in their aura - even if thousands of miles distant.

It is known that these thoughts often come back to the originator, so it is worthwhile to always have good thoughts of others - and of yourself.

If you do not like the behavior of another, then send thoughts of how you would like them to behave; if enough people do this, a change might be effected.

If a political leader is involved, this may be more effective than the ballot-box - and the desired result may occur sooner !

Remember that such leaders are subject to the influence of those around them or otherwise involved in decisions being made - so send the thoughts to 'all concerned', not just the figurehead.

Thought precedes Action

This may seem to be contradicted by our 'fight or flight' actions resulting from emotional triggers (the thought may be sub-conscious), by the action of tides (which may be following the laws of gravity - perhaps made by a 'higher level of thought'), and by seemingly automatic happenings (installed as programs, themselves formed from thoughts).

Certainly a lot of thought goes into developing any new idea, often from a number of people. More thought is then given to the best way of getting the wanted results from the idea - such as materials needed, manufacturing process, marketing aids, sales efforts, financial implications, and other applicable requirements.

This applies to going on a holiday, baking a cake, handling your correspondence, meeting new people, taking the dog for a walk, going to sleep, or any other activity. The thoughts will differ, but all that are needed will exist - together with thoughts that arose, but were discarded for whatever reason.

The initial idea will be a thought to do or make something; perhaps this will be sketched, or notes made - a two dimensional image. The intermediate steps and the final result may be visualized - now three dimensions. Then, if all seems correct, you may do what is needed to achieve or make the result.

The greater the detail that goes into this thought process, the better the chances of success.

Help from 'Upstairs'

You may find that you get thoughts in your Mind that you did not originate, but help you with the success of your project. Perhaps you are tapping into the 'Cosmic Store' of information and knowledge.

There is a well established principle: 'Like attracts Like'. This occurs with your thoughts about whatever you are trying to achieve - not only in your endeavours to make something, but also in your personal life.

If you are depressed in any way, you will usually find that the people around you are also depressed - often in the same way. For 'depressed' you can substitute any other description, good or 'not good'.

You are the captain in charge of your thoughts. If you put a lot of effort into changing negative thoughts into positive ones, this will happen - but it may take time. Using the EFT and similar procedures you can speed this process, and also improve your health.

The Secret

This is the name of a film, available on DVD, that you may have seen - it explains that if you really want something, visualize the desired result, and put your emotions into this action, then 'The Universe' will provide. It tells the story of many people who have done this with great success.

If you continually put your efforts into thinking 'the very best' then that will be the end result - that is what you attract.

Do not fall into the trap of thinking that you know more than 'Upstairs' - visualize and put emotions into the desired result, NOT into 'How this Happens'.

You may think that you need to win the lottery - 'Upstairs' may have a better way of getting the money that you need to come to you.

Notice that the accent is on 'what you need' - not on just what you want. In the same context, do not limit yourself ! Do not think of just $100 to solve an immediate problem - 'Upstairs' may know that you need $1000 to 'get on your feet' again, or even more if you are open to using it to help others for a good purpose. Ask for 'all that you need to have a good life'.

'Need, NOT Greed' is the motto - if you are just being greedy, then you will probably attract others who are greedy, not anything that is useful to you in any substantial way.

Quality of Thought

'Be careful of what you request - you may get it!' and find that although it fits your description, it is not suitable ! Do not ask for 'a Cadillac' - the one that you get may be on its way to the scrap heap.

Be clear and precise - define the model, year, colour, that it be in excellent working condition, that it remain in excellent working condition for all the time that you own it (and say how long the minimum period), that it never gives you any large repair bills, that you and your family will always be safe in it.

Remember the ancient story of King Midas - who wished that 'All that he touched then turned into gold'. Have you tried eating gold ?

There is always 'enough to go round' - but it may require effort on your own part to make this happen. Wealth is not going to come to someone who just thinks of being rich, without making any effort to improve his/her abilities and skills, or fails to put the needed physical energy into achievement.

For example, you are not going to meet your desired partner if you spend all your time watching television ! You must, at the very least, get out and meet other people, and make yourself presentable in all ways.

'No Harm to Others'

Remember that your thoughts attract similar thoughts - and that these can become actions. So if you think negatively about any other person, the chances are that you will suffer in the same way.

There is no harm in wanting to be as rich as another - if this is held as an aim for yourself. But to hold jealousy or envy, or wish that they lose their riches, is to attract disaster to your own self.

Any thought that you have for the detriment of others is like casting a spell. Some people have the skill to do this effectively, and usually they suffer a similar fate later.

If you do not have the skill, the result may not be effective on others - but can surely affect you, who asked for it to happen. Be safe, and ensure that all of your thoughts are kind and positive.

It helps to remember that none of us are perfect - 'There is good in the worst of us, and bad in the best of us'. Robin Hood stole from the rich to give to the poor - the opposite of the policies of many business co-operations and some governments.

You may recall a number of prominent religious leaders who called for donations for the general good - but really meant the 'General in Charge', themselves ! Thankfully these cases are few - but they do happen.

The Power of Love

We have discussed the thoughts - now let us have a deeper look into how we can reinforce these to obtain manifestation - to make them materialize.

The strongest of all feelings is Love. The Eskimo have about fifty words for snow, to adequately describe all its textures. We, however, have only one word for Love - including all its variations.

Love of money, of power, of certain foods, of various drinks, of pretty clothes. Sexual attraction (I love you !), anticipation of a pleasant happening (I'd love to go there !), and musical appreciation (I love that music !) are examples.

The real Love, 'True Holy Love', is doing your best to help others for the good of all; this does not include helping them to realize greed or do things which are detrimental or harmful to any others in any way.

'Others' includes all life forms, all the Creations of the 'Holy Creator in Love of All Things, in All Places, in All Dimensions, in All Times'.

This may be the best description of the 'One God' - not just the God of Humans, but of 'All That Is'. Personally, I do not believe that any 'Good God' wants to be worshipped - what is really wanted is to help him/her to care for all His/Her Creations, to give them respect and Love.

Is this what we do by polluting the earth ? By poisoning plants and insects ? By not caring about the side effects of actions that we take - or even purposefully hurting other life forms ? *"Do unto others as you would have done to you".*

Gratitude for the benefits that we receive, as a genuine feeling, does encourage more benefits to be given. If one is ungrateful, the reaction may be *"Why should we bother with him ? Let us help those who are thankful instead."*

This can often be recognized in human relationships - at home, at work, and at play. The old wisdom 'As Above, So Below' may be reversible - 'As Below, So Above', since we are all just different aspects of the same creation.

When we seek to do 'whatever' for the general good, to help others, then we are acting in Love. Action is far more important than words. How often do people say one thing, and then do something else, or the opposite to their 'promise' ?

This type of behavior is not restricted to politicians !

If the intent is to help others, not just one's own self, then 'Upstairs' is far more likely to put great effort in helping the manifestation of what is desired.

The Effect of Emotions

After Love, next most powerful is the effect of putting a great deal of emotion into your request.

As discussed with emotional triggers, any very strong emotion attaches great importance to whatever is being thought, and so your sub-consciousness puts more effort into attracting and manifesting things that are associated with the thought.

This could be called an 'emotional attractor', and seems to have a lot of similarity with an 'emotional trigger' - guiding you to do what is needed to assist with the manifestation.

Failure to build an emotional attractor may mean that the chances of success are greatly reduced. You have not strongly indicated the importance of your desire to your sub-conscious mind-brain team.

In this context, the emotion to be attached must be positive ! Any hate, anger, or greed involved will attract those negative reactions to you - to your own detriment.

Attach happiness, joy, freedom from negativity (of whatever description), and the emotions associated with Love itself.

Be Sensual !

Use all your senses to reinforce your desires - to implement the realization that 'what you desire' has already happened !

You may not yet be aware of 'it' in the physical world, but your thoughts have already started to make it happen in the world of thoughts !

... So visualize yourself enjoying the desired result.
... See yourself using whatever it is with beneficial results.
... Imagine how your life has changed for the good.
... Picture how others get benefit from your manifestation.

Bring your other senses into use, too:

... Feel the beneficial changes that happen to you.
... Feel how these changes help others.
... Feel how others appreciate these changes.
... Hear other people congratulating you.
... Taste the fruits of success.
... Smell the aroma that goes with a successful person.
... Touch all you can with these benefits.
... Know that all is now well.

The more effort that you put into this, the stronger becomes the attraction generated, and the more likely the successful result.

Magical Ceremony

The actions just described are very similar to any magical ceremony. The main difference is that it is not just you yourself doing all the work, but a group of like-minded people.

You are achieving magical results - things that others believe cannot be done by ordinary people, only by magicians or other 'special people' such as priests.

The ceremonial part of this is the reinforcement of a thought or a collection of thoughts by repetition - a church ceremony, a witches coven, a Healing circle, a political rally, a sports meeting, or anywhere the routine is repeated with the same intent.

Of course, at a sports meeting you probably have opposing thoughts - and those of people who are distant will still have effect. This may also happen at a corporate meeting, since the attendees may have diverse agendas.

The larger the number of Human Beings that participate, the more friends from 'Upstairs' will be attracted - and they may well be able to do things with you that you cannot do alone.

Be sure to attract 'Good Friends' ! That is the 'Real Magic'.

You are a Magician !

You can make things happen ! You can improve life for others - and yourself !

The greatest impediment is the belief that you cannot do something. Your own beliefs, 'stuck' in your mind-brain programming, are very effective in sabotaging anything that is contrary to themselves.

When you actually force the first step, you start to open your mind-brain team to a new belief - that you <u>can</u> do it !

...   If you do not make the effort, you cannot succeed.
...   If you do not ask, you may not get.
...   If you do not succeed at first, do it again.
...   Perseverance pays ! Do it NOW !

Any time is a good time. The best time is when you are most closely co-operating with your sub-conscious - when you are in the half-awake/half-asleep state, going to sleep or awakening, and especially when you wake for a short time in mid-sleep.

Develop a routine, your magical ceremony, that you work through at these times - like an affirmation, but more extensive, more powerful, and so more likely to succeed.

At these times you have alpha and/or theta brainwave patterns. There are many methods of achieving this same state when awake, so if you develop the skill of using these methods you can then put even more effort into manifesting your desire.

Subliminal messages were used in advertising - short flashes on television of a message, which did not register upon your conscious self, but were absorbed by your sub-conscious self.

These have now been banned in most countries; they were very effective, but were considered an abuse on the populace. Does this means that they should now be reserved only for use by governments ?

You can achieve a similar effect by using reminders of various types. These must be specifically associated with your desires, either in an obvious way such as spelling it in words or displaying it in pictures, or in a less obvious manner such as a special graphic.

Such a graphic must be drawn by you while thinking of your desire, and include symbols which you directly associate with your desire and its aspects and benefits.

It should be such that other people are unaware of its meaning - it is understood by you alone, and thus has 'extra special' meaning for you.

These reminders are excellent when placed so that you see them when going to sleep or awakening, since they remind you about your ceremony, and to 'do it now'.

They are also very effective in places where you relax - including your office where you may day-dream, your workplace where your attention may wander, or where you eyes go to get relief from television adverts. They will form a focus for your thoughts.

In all this, the strongest manifestation is when you use your Intuitive Heart-Mind-Brain team, and not rely just on your egoistic mind-brain team.

Do it NOW,
Do it with LOVE.

"I don't mind,
You don't matter"
Defining Mind and Matter

It is a Matter of Form

It is my understanding that 'All that Is' is made of the same 'Baby Energies' or 'Lights' doing different three (or more) dimensional 'dances' at various speeds to form everything, and doing so in families, teams, teams of families, and families of teams - the complexity of the dances growing with the size of the numbers of dancers involved.

Physicists know that atoms are made of sub-atomic particles of various form, and that electrons are there, then not there - then somewhere else an electron appears, perhaps a replacement.

It seems that they are moving in and out of the physical dimension - and so into a different dimension, perhaps operating at a different speed, if this is the difference between dimensions.

Not only are these dances performed to form matter, but also to form thoughts and auric patterns, and doing this in all levels of existence, in all dimensions.

'As Above, So Below' implies that this is the 'substance' of 'Energy Beings' at all levels, including Angels, Elementals, Spirits, etc.

Sub-atomic Particles

When examining the way that sub-atomic particles operate, physicists find that different particles can be recognized by their attributes: the form of the dance that they make, and the effect of that dance upon others - such dances being consistent for any particular form of particle.

Patterns can be described as mathematical rules and formulae - intelligence must be involved in making these, to define the basic steps, and the ways that these are joined to form more complicated equations.

This has been recognized by mystics as the basis of 'Sacred Geometry', and demonstrated by computer users experimenting with Mandelbrot pattern growth.

The Dancers

If the idea is correct that everything is made of these dancers, then they must intrinsically 'know' what to do, or that they follow a 'Dance Leader' - who must know what is required for a dance.

In either case this implies that all who are involved in such dances have the ability to think (what do I do next ?), to act (I do the dance), to feel (does the dance feel correct ?), and perhaps to Love (I Love to do a dance which is beneficial to others !).

If so, then each Light and Baby Energy is a Being in its own right ! Even more important (for us) is the understanding that 'We are All the Same' - and so can communicate with others like us. Not just other human beings, but with 'All that Is' - 'Above' as well as 'Below'.

How can we use this ability ?

Vibrational Patterns

These are the dances made - the vibrational patterns being the small movement of a microscopic (or even far smaller) dance.

Any thought that we have is itself a vibrational pattern - and wave studies have shown that when waves meet, their patterns are affected, the new patterns embodying the contributory patterns.

This is the basis of holography, which proceeds to 'untangle' the combinations to obtain copies of the original contributory patterns, using the knowledge that each tiny part of the combination has its own picture of the whole - including the original patterns.

Therefore it follows that whenever we send a thought, we have an effect on the recipients - whether or not the recipients are those that we intended.

The more precisely that we direct our thoughts, the higher the concentration of the thought that can be expected to be received by the intended recipient.

Improving the Environment

By propagating good thoughts, we will improve our immediate environment - at home, work, or play. The more people who do this, the stronger will be the effect - and since Emoto and Backster have demonstrated that water and plants are responsive (and we know this is true for animals) then our thoughts can be expected to have an effect on the total environment - even throughout the world.

Unfortunately there are a lot of people having 'not good' thoughts of various types, so we may have to work very hard to make any substantive change on a large scale - but every little effort helps !

Home First !

We can expect to get the best results when we work on a small scale - on ourselves, our family, our working environment, and our community.

We ourselves are influenced by the thoughts and actions of others - and especially how we respond !

It is our response which activates reaction within our own Being, so the less negative emotion that we attach to the thoughts and actions of others, the less we are affected.

Love is the strongest force, the greatest power - so when something happens that could be detrimental to us, just send thoughts of Love to those involved, to help them be healed of their problems.

Energy Healing

We do not like being hurt. If 'As Above, So Below' is correct, then this applies to all life forms, which are all made of energies.

Often it is those who have been hurt in some way who 'take it out' on others. It may be that the energies in those who are causing problems have been hurt, and that they need to be Healed.

This can apply to the energies within ourselves - who may be the cause or effect of hurts. So sending Love and Healing to yourself, and to all the energies in your total Being, can effect Healing of yourself - and your problems and illnesses.

By sending this Love and Healing you are changing the vibrational pattern of your components such as your cells and organs - changing them for better, and helping them to Heal.

By blessing your food, you increase its 'Life Force', its 'Love Energy' - when you eat it, it is more beneficial for you !

Making 'Sanjeevini' Medicine

Dr Emoto has shown that water is responsive to thought, even changing its physical structure according to the thoughts applied.

Since water is the major component of our body cells, any beneficial vibrational pattern that we apply to the water that is in these cells will itself be beneficial to ourselves.

This also applies to the water that we drink, which will go to these cells; this can be used as a method of changing normal water into a medicine !

This diagram is a 'Sanjeevini Card', developed in India and placed on the Internet - see www.Sanjeevini.org for full instructions.

BPS 52 **Sanathana Sai** Bone Marrow **Sanjeevini**

You can download these cards for the Healing of 60 different body parts and 186 diseases !

Some years ago some similar symbols were put on the internet from a source in the USA - but intense legal action by the US drug companies and medical associations forced their removal.

Luckily, these Sanjeevini symbols are outside the jurisdiction of the authorities in the USA.

These were developed by Poornima Nagpal , who was guided over a period of 8 months to make these remedies, with the intent of helping poor people who could not afford medicines to have an effective cure. There are many testamonials to their effectiveness.

We can consider two dimensional symbols as 'maps' of the three dimensional dances - not the 'real thing', but a representation. Notwithstanding this, they are effective - they work !

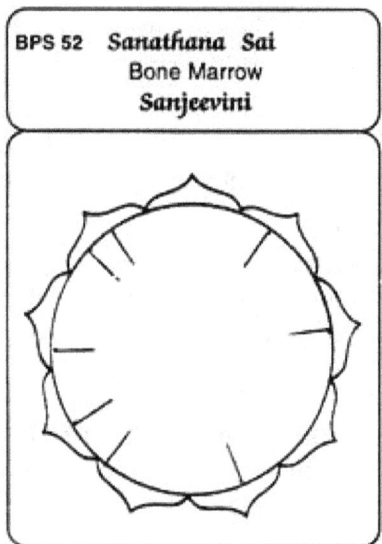

One way to use these Sanjeevini symbols is to select the needed symbol, and place it under a glass of water for 15 seconds - very simple !

The symbol puts the needed vibrational pattern for Healing into the water - an analysis of the water would not show this, since the vibrational pattern is 'too subtle' to be ascertained by physical examination. This is just like a homeopathic remedy.

The web page includes a manual which explains other methods of use, including how more than one symbol can be combined, and the use of carriers other than water.

Making your own Medicine

Bill Askin is a trapper from northern Alberta, highly skilled in the Silva Mind Method and in Dowsing - he introduced Raymon Grace, a leading Silva teacher and internationally known Shaman, to Dowsing.

Bill has developed a very simple method of demonstrating the use of one's Power of Thought with a Pendulum:

1. Take a glass of water, and taste it - remember the taste.
2. Use your Pendulum to make anti-clockwise rotations over the glass of water, asking that *"All things not good for me be removed from this water"*.
3. Taste the water again - it probably has a better taste.
4. Use your Pendulum to make clockwise rotations over the glass of water, asking that *"All things needed for my good health be installed into this water"*.
5. Taste the water again - it probably has an even better taste, and is now medicine designed just for you ! Drink it all.

Remember to express your gratitude to all involved in so helping you to have such good water !

Do not expect to be completely Healed at the first sip that you take - like most medicines, time is needed to be fully effective, and further doses may be needed.

People who have done this experiment are amazed at the way the taste changes, even without noticing any immediate medicinal effects. Experiment yourself - unlike most man-made medicines, there will not be any side-effects, so you cannot be hurt.

If you want the very best medicine, say when installing with a clockwise rotation: *"I Bless this water with 'True Holy Love, Namaste', with 'Blessing 995', and with 'Healing 997'. I send my personal thanks, my personal gratitude, and my personal Love, to all who help in this ceremony".*

Remember to be sincere when doing any of this work !

This last blessing can be used with all that you eat or drink - better still, Bless 'All that is Consumed' for a greater effect.

Experimenting with Thought

This needs another person to help you !

Imagine, in your mind, that you build a wall along a particular line; imaging the bricks, etc., being placed strongly and securely - make it as high as you like, use materials other than brick if you so prefer.

As with all Mind work, the more emotional energy that you put into this visualization, the greater will be the effect.

Now ask your helper to see if s/he can feel anything as the wall is approached ! Can you feel it yourself ?

You may find success in building a wall (or similar) to keep animals on or off your property, as a barrier against rodents, or a shield against mosquitoes.

What you build is not in the physical dimension; but since thought precedes action, and it is considered to be real by the thinking processes of the life forms involved, it works.

When making a shield, you must have a clear intent of its exact purpose, where it is to be located, and the time for it to be active - and make sure that the purpose is described in a positive way, that it is beneficial, without harm to others.

If you find that the shield that you make does not work as well as you hoped, ask your Heart how it can be improved - and accept the advice given by the very first thought that 'pops' into your Mind.

One big advantage of such a barrier is that it does not harm the life forms involved, such as rats, mice, or mosquitoes - it just keeps them away.

You may find that the power of a shield drops with time, and needs to be reinforced - for you to put more of your personal energy into it, with your Love and Gratitude for the help given.

Such a shield does not have to be fixed in any one spot - it can be linked to a person or object. You can build a mosquito shield around yourself, or place protection around your car.

A case has been reported concerning the effects of such a screen around a car - the owner placed a shield of blue light around the car with the intention that the car would be invisible to police.

It worked ! The car was rammed by a police car on an emergency mission - the police driver did not see the car !

You can place a protective shield around a home or other property, and fill inside the shield with Peace, Harmony, and True Holy Love, Namaste.

Protect One Self !

Have you found that when you are with certain people, they really seem to enjoy your company - but afterwards you feel drained ? Some people do suck energy from others !

To overcome this, visualize a protective shell around you that prevents your energy from being sucked or drained by other life forms (not by only humans) - doing this as a safety precaution.

Do not make it so that it stops all energy, since then you would not get the incoming good energy that you need.

You do not have to specify the shape or colours of the shield - ask your Guardian Angel (or other Spiritual Helpers) to make it and place it in position.

Often 'Upstairs' may need you to put some physical energy into anything that you do in other dimensions.

They may not use it as it is, but transform it into something else - physical energy is quite strong, and using the energy provided helps 'Upstairs' to do more.

A simple clapping of your hands may be all that is needed; perhaps it is meant to help you understand that you must help yourself, not just rely on others.   Remember to thank all who so help you !

You will probably find that the energy sucking people do not relish your company so much - they cannot steal your energy, perhaps the main reason for being friendly with you !

You can take similar steps to prevent or reduce harassment or other such problems at your home or workplace.

Mind over Matter

These experiments will probably have helped you to realize that you have great 'Mind Power' - all humans have this, even if they are not so aware.

As described in the film 'The Secret', there are many 'energies' in Creation that are waiting for a good job - a job that is beneficial, that gives them a chance to help others.

The human Mind has the ability to call on these resources, and to work with other levels of 'Being-ness' to improve life for all - not just other humans !

Our thoughts can identify what is needed, visualize the completed design, and take steps to 'make it so' - not only in the physical dimension, but as we have seen, also in the dimension of thought.

When we 'plant a thought' it will grow according to the nutrients supplied - including the comparable thoughts of others. The more people who think in the same way, the greater the likelihood that the thought will flourish.

The greatest of all nutrients is Love; as with the light from the sun, some of this is needed for growth - and lots of Love will enable good, strong growth. There is little difference between 'Love' and 'Life' - as written, or in reality.

Viciousness, violence, greed, selfishness, and similar negativity are all like herbicides that have a detrimental effect - perhaps even killing the plant.

> ... **Have Good Intent**
> ... **Work with your Heart**
> ... **Do it with Love**
> ... **Visualize it has Happened**
> ... **Add Positive Emotions**
> ... **Feel Good about the Result**
> ... **Express your Gratitude**
> ... **Send Love to 'All who Helped'**

Every Noxious Energy does not result in Cancer;
Every Case of Cancer found was in a Noxious Energy zone.

Käthe Bachler and European Medical Researchers

More on Noxious Energies

One aspect of Health that is only now receiving any recognition in North America is the effect of earth and water energies. The original Feng Shui included the location and identification of these 'dragons', but the loss of understanding over the years has caused many practitioners to just 'go by the book' without using the needed Dowsing skills.

In Europe the builders of ancient structures (like Stonehenge) and of cathedrals were aware of these energies, and chose sites with the utmost care.

But even good energies can be harmful (and so noxious to humans, animals, insects, plants, etc.) if they are too strong for the individual or the exposure is too long.

Humans, dogs, horses, cows, sheep, and pigs find most of these energies noxious - so if your dog loves to sleep in your chair or on your bed it is probably clear of these energies.

But if a cat chooses such spots, beware - cars, ants, and bees love the concentrations. Bee keepers try to place their hives on energy crossings to get increased honey yields.

The energies themselves are not the disease - their noxious effect lowers our resistance and vitality so that diseases, etc., that we would normally overcome are able to 'take root' and harm us.

German medical doctors, including Dr Curry and Dr Hartmann, investigated these noxious energies in modern times, as well as Gustav Baron von Pohl.

Studies were made by Dowsers of where noxious energies existed, were plotted on maps, and then compared with deaths from cancer - with excellent correlation.

As a result there are places in Europe where geopathic studies are required before hospitals, schools, and other institutions are built.

We have already seen some of the cases examined by Käthe Bachler - cases where extended sitting or sleeping caused sudden infant deaths, inattention at school, and diseases such as cancer, arthritis, and heart problems. (For more details see page 165)

In all these cases it needed only to change the seat or bed to avoid 'bad spots' - and when this was done the health problems disappeared !

Russian experience concurs - Dr Melnikov, Director of the Medical and Ecological Department of the Geo-Ecological Centre in St. Petersburg, reports a 5 year study looking at a 5 mile stretch of the city for geopathic zones in which 100 of 1,000 houses were labelled as being 'cancer houses'.

Hospital and medical records were checked; 90% of oncological cases occurred in the zones, including direct correlation with leukemia in children.

Examination of Traffic Records showed a corresponding high rate of traffic accidents in the streets within these zones.

Locating and Evaluating Noxious Energies

Location of earth energies is best done by Dowsing - which works in all planes of existence, in all dimensions.

Accordingly I have designed a Logarithmic Numerical Chart specially for the Dowsing of the values encountered in handling noxious energies.

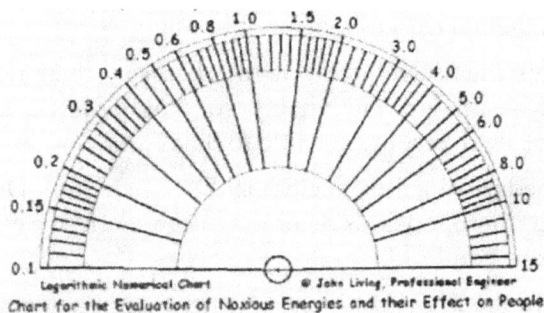

Logarithmic Numerical Chart   © John Living, Professional Engineer
Chart for the Evaluation of Noxious Energies and their Effect on People

Unity (the value of 1.0 on the chart) represents the **'Average input of Beneficial Life Force/Energy that you receive in an hour from all sources'** - or 'Hourly Input' for short.

Extremely durable Vinyl-Plastic business cards printed with this chart are available (with a glass bead Pendulum) from the Holistic Intuition Society. To purchase one, see our web site: **www.in2it.ca/tools.htm** - *or see our other contact information in this book.*

To use the chart, ask your Heart-Mind-Brain team to signal the amount of your 'Hourly Input' that would be used by you if you were to remain in the spot below the centre point of the card.

In most places this will be in the range from 0.2 to 0.4, signifying that it is a good position for you. Any value below 1.0 indicates that you have a net gain of beneficial energy, but the closer to 1.0 the less spare energy is available for other normal activities.

Any value greater than 1.0 means that you would have a net loss of energy if remaining in that place. The greater the value, the more detrimental is the noxious energy. Any position giving a reading above 0.4 is best avoided.

You can go around your bed or chair (and elsewhere in the room) to get an idea of where the energy lines are running, and then plot the values on a sketch to give you a 'map' of the energetic situation.

Using this map you can decide the best location for your chair or bed. If you get a reading of 5 or more at any point, it may be the effect of a 'Lost Soul' - so ask your Heart to get Angelic Assistance for the Lost Soul, or take any other appropriate action.

Then ask your Heart if this has been done, and if so then recheck the values at that place - they may well now be at normal good levels.

If you wish to identify the underlying causes of any noxious energy, you can ask your Heart to indicate YES or NO to the various types of causes.

The order of asking about depletion energies may best be:
1. Earthbound Energies (Souls, Spirits - of all types) - since they are so strong that their effect 'blankets out' other readings.
2. Curses - because they are usually covering a very large area.
3. EMF Radiations - often being noxious over a large area (from transformers), or very local (electric appliances).
4. Noxious Water Veins - they wander across the grids.
5. Curry Lines - easily identifiable, known spacing.
6. Pollution in Hartmann Grid - perhaps more common in rural areas, due to unbalanced electrical distribution systems.
7. Other Sources - and ask as guided by your Intuition.

Methods of Transmuting Noxious Energies

There are very simple, exceedingly effective, and remarkably inexpensive ways to transmute noxious energies to become beneficial.

Earthbound Energies

If you get a reading of 5 or more at any point, it may be the effect of a 'Lost Soul' - so ask your Heart to get Angelic Assistance for the Lost Soul, or take any other appropriate action.

Then ask your Heart if this has been done, and if so then recheck the values at that place - they may well now be at normal good levels.

Curses

These may not have been placed intentionally ! Just 'wishing' that 'something bad' happen to a person, family, or community could be the cause. This may have happened many centuries (or even millennia) ago, and the person who placed the curse may have departed.

The energies involved in any curse do not like their job, but are 'stuck with it' since nobody has freed them. This is a job that you can do very easily - just tell *"All involved in all curses in all times on this land and buildings are now free ! So now go 'into the Light' !"* and ask the Angelic Forces to help them on their way. Note: 'times' is plural !

EMF Radiations

Gary Skillen, a past president of the Canadian Society of Dowsers, has found that crushed calcite crystals are excellent for absorbing the EMF radiations.

I experimented with placing thought forms of such crystals at a few electrical outlets and in front of my sound system, and found that they worked well; but after a couple of days the effect returned, so I asked why this happened. I was told *"We are overloaded. We need to be grounded."* - so I placed a grounding thought form in the piles of metaphysical calcite crystals, and they are doing a good job again.

The effectiveness of the calcite crystals seems to be enhanced by placing a sodalite crystal on top; if you placed a thought form of calcite crystals, then use another thought form for the sodalite (or add it to the calcite thought form).

How do you place a 'Thought Form' ? You just picture it being built - using your Heart-Mind-Brain team ! You explain the job, the length of time for the job to be done, charge the energies involved to do the job by sending them 'True Holy Love', and send your gratitude and thanks to all involved in this task.

Ray Machell reports on his testing of this method:

"The first item to be cleared was my new 21" computer monitor. Before starting I measured the distance that the monitor radiated energy that was detrimental to me. It was 64", much more than I expected.

With thought I placed crushed calcite crystals around the base, the edges of the screen, and on top of the monitor.

Measurement showed that the radiation had been reduced to 40". I then imagined a sodalite crystal on top of each pile of calcite crystals - the radiation was now reduced to only 18" !

I then grounded each pile of crystals by thinking that each was connected by wire to an imaginary ground rod driven into the earth. Incredible - the radiation was now only $2\frac{1}{2}$" !!

In all this procedure I asked permission by Dowsing to do the work, indicated the purpose of the request and the length of time needed to be effective - in this case the time that I owned the monitor. Upon completion, I gave thanks to all involved."

Noxious Water Veins

These seem to be noxious because they get loaded with 'bad thoughts' - water is very receptive to thoughts, as demonstrated by Dr Emoto in his book 'Message from Water', which shows the various patterns formed in ice crystals when subjected to written notes, different types of music, and homeopathic remedies.

First locate the vein of water running deep below your room, and find the direction of flow - also by Dowsing - just ask !

Now go as far upstream as possible, and bless the vein and the water that it carries: *"I Bless with 'True Holy Love' this water vein and all the water that it carries, and ask the help of 'The System' and the 'Angelic Forces' to Heal this water vein and all the water that it carries for all time, and to change its effect to become beneficial for all life."*

Curry Lines

These may not be seen by clairvoyants, so are often ignored by people who rely on their 'second sight', which seems to operate in the 'Astral Plane'. The Curry Grid exists in a higher plane of existence - but has effect on lower planes.

The grid runs NW-SE and NE-SW, the grid lines alternating YIN and YANG, forming vortices (like miniature tornados) at the grid junctions.

The strength of the lines varies, similar to a city's road system - most being like residential roads with acceptable strength, with collector roads at intervals which can be noxious, and with occasional highways of very high noxicity. If you sleep on a highway, expect to get 'run over' !

To Heal these Curry lines, Bless them in a similar way to the Blessing for noxious water veins.

As an example, the following was reported by Gary Skillen:

While teaching how to locate these zones we identified a Curry crossing point.

Each student took turns to stand on the point and described the effect on their bodies. Some felt sick to their stomachs, others tipped over or got a tingling sensation.

Suddenly a thought came to me to use Dowsing to find out how detrimental this crossing was to humans.

On a scale from 1 (no problem) to 10 (most detrimental) this crossing was at 10. My next thought was:

"Maybe this Curry line has its own consciousness, its own awareness of itself; and is suffering as well ! And if I acknowledge the fact that it has its own awareness with respect, perhaps I can communicate with the energies involved".

I then asked:

"Are you detrimental to your own self ?" YES

"Do you want to remain detrimental ?" NO

"Do you want to change to being beneficial ?" YES

"Do I have permission to help you change to being beneficial ?" YES

"So be it !"

I took my Pendulum and allowed it to swing in the direction necessary to make the change - it swung clockwise for about 2 to 3 minutes, and then stopped.

I asked *"Is the correction made ?"* YES.

Each student then took turns standing on the same spot and reporting how they felt - some were apprehensive about repeating their previous experience, but all were pleasantly surprised !

This same crossing point now gave them more energy - and it was beneficial !

Pollution in Hartmann Grid

This seems to be caused by 'out of balance' electrical currents that are using the ground as their return path to 'source', and are most noticeable in rural areas.

I suggest that you treat them in the same way as other EMF energies, using grounded thought forms of calcite and sodalite. Metal rods driven into their flow path may also be used to divert the flow - or even the placing of thought forms instead of real ones !

An alternative way is to place a thought form of a solid 'Good Gold' ring around the house, to act as a 'traffic circle' for the enegies involved. This method may also be used for energies in the Curry Grid - using a separate ring.

Fun, Not Hard Work !

Improving one's abilities and skills should be pleasant and enjoyable - not tedious or overly difficult.

Let us look at some ways that this can be done.

Everyday Opportunities

... Guess who is calling when the telephone rings.

... Hold a letter and imagine what is written.

... Visualize the colour of clothes that will be worn by someone you are to meet.

... Estimate the number of people who will attend a meeting.

... Ask your car if there is any problem. What comes to your mind immediately ? Perhaps nothing, if all is fine !

... Feel the atmosphere of all rooms that you enter.

... Visualize the look of a person you will be meeting for the first time.

... In a store, note when you enter a queue at the pay counter, estimate how many minutes until you leave the store.

Note that selecting lucky numbers for the lottery is not listed - it may work for you, but has not worked for me !

In all these examples, practice improves your skill - you may not succeed the first time, but every time you do one of these exercises you improve your ability.

Sector Selection

Perhaps the most important information that is needed by any person is which of the 'Soul Senses' is their strongest, since it pays to improve what you have before expending effort on something new.

Marking a paper with sectors enables you to display many different choices; you are not limited to the four shown here, but it is best not to have so many that they become crowded together.

Usually you will have one sector allocated to 'other' - in case you have not listed the best choice for you.

If this 'other' is then selected, be aware of the very first thought that 'pops' into your head, make a new selection chart which includes that choice, and repeat the process.

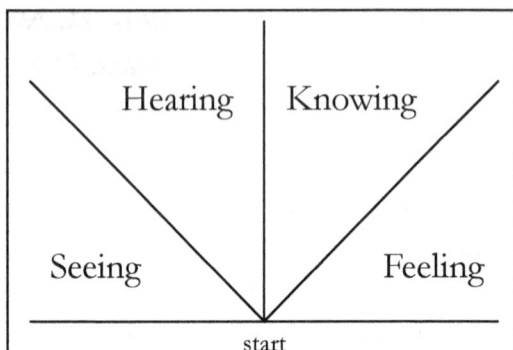

Hearing   Knowing

Seeing   Feeling

start

You could have listed possible places to go on your next holiday, employment types or employers for consideration, addressees of a possible next home, food to be eaten, which person to hire, which car to buy, or any other choices in your daily decisions.

There are a number of ways to make the selection; hold the thought of the question in your mind, and ask your Heart for the answer.

Then you can look at the selections shown and be aware of where your eye 'homes'; just know for some reason which is the best; rub your finger gently over the list and feel if it 'sticks' in any particular sector; or use your Pendulum by holding it over the 'start' and noting where it points when it starts to swing.

You can then repeat this asking if you have another Soul Sense that is very strong - people often have one that is extremely strong, and another which is very strong.

A variation is to make a list of items (vitamins, allergies, foods, holiday places, possible employers, etc), then feel if any item 'sticks' to indicate its selection.

You can also point to each in turn (a pen or pencil as a pointer is fine) and hold your Pendulum in your other hand, asking for a signal when 'gold is found'.

Remember that in a number of cases you may be interested in more than one 'golden nugget' - your body may need more than one vitamin or other supplement.

Map Locating

You can use the above method on a map - it has square sectors, marking the co-ordinates. Here you can move in the north-south direction asking *"Is the XXX in this line of east-west squares ?"*, and then moving to these squares in sequence and asking *"Is XXX in this square ?"*.

When a square is chosen, you can sub-divide it into smaller squares and repeat this procedure to narrow down the location.

If XXX was gold or water, remember that there are minute quantities of gold in most soils, and that soils that are damp contain water.

You should be far more specific in your search criteria before spending money to dig a gold mine or drill a well !

If you are seeking a missing person, remember that you will probably not succeed if they do not want to be found; you also find it best to have some sort of connection to them - a photograph, piece of their hair, or some of their clothing.

This use of a connection is called 'using a witness' - and can greatly improve your accuracy.

Card Guessing Game

You will need a deck of playing cards, pen/pencil and paper to keep score. You will use your Intuition to determine if the next card drawn is red or black suited, later to identify the suite, and finally the value. You can use your Soul Senses or Pendulum

Remove jokers and shuffle the pack of cards (the deck).

Ask your Intuition *"Is the next card in a red suite ?"* - write down your forecast: R (for red) if you got YES, or B (for black) if you got NO for an answer.

Draw the card from the top of the deck, and write another R or B (next to the letter indicating your forecast) to show the result. Repeat with the next card, writing your forecast and the result on the next line.

Why ? Because when you start getting these correct, your Intuition may start playing a game with you - quite often you will find that the forecast will not be for the top card on the deck, but the one below it ! Sometimes even for the one below that !

By writing the forecast and result side-by-side and below each other, you will be able to spot if the result column matches the forecast column, or is one or two cards 'out of step' !

As a variation, after you ask the colour, if red ask *"Is it a Heart ?"* and if YES write H after your colour forecast letter (write D for diamond if you got NO); or if black ask about a Spade - and write S for spade or C for Club.

You can carry this even further to find the card value. Ask your Intuition *"Is the next card an ace ?"* - if so, write A on a new line; if not, ask *"Is the next card a picture card ?"* and if YES, ask *"Is the next card a (king, queen, or jack) ?"* - whichever you 'feel in your mind' is the best to ask about.

Do not get rigid in this, such as always asking the same sequence - go with your feeling, which may be your Intuition guiding you.

If you got NO to the card being an ace or a picture card, then you ask *"Is the next card a (any number from 2 to 10) ?"* - whichever you 'feel in your mind' is the best to ask about.

If you get NO, then use the method that computer programs use to find a solution: ask *"Is the value greater than 5 ?"* - if the answer is YES, then it must be between 6 and 10, so split the difference and ask *"Is the value greater than 8 ?"* - if YES, ask about 9 - another YES means it must be a 10, NO indicates it is a 9 since it is greater than 8 but not more than 9 !

Split the difference in the same way if you got NO to being greater than 5 - it must be between 2 and 5, so check greater than 3, etc.

You can combine all these ways to forecast the suite and value of the cards ! Use this for fun - not to bet your savings at the casino !

Bored, with nothing to do ?

Play this game, not just to pass the time, but to improve your Intuitive abilities.

Shaking a Dice

You need a dice with a throwing cup, perhaps your Pendulum.

Shake the dice in the thrower and then place the thrower on a table, open end down, to hide the dice.

First Method - Counting:

Ask your Pendulum to give as many circles as are spots on the top surface of the dice.

At the start you may find that you are one or two numbers out - perhaps due to your Pendulum starting and stopping its swing motion.

As you get accustomed to working with your Pendulum, you will get a better idea of which swings to count.

Second Method - Splitting Values:

Ask your Pendulum *"Are there [any number from 1 to 6] spots on the top surface of the dice ?"* - whichever number you 'feel in your mind' is the best to ask about. Remember that if you do not specify which surface, you could get answers that may be correct - but not what you intended.

If you get NO, then use the method that computer programs use to find a solution: ask *"Is the value greater than 3 ?"* - if the answer is YES, then it must be between 4 and 6, so split the difference and ask *"Is the value greater than 5 ?"* - YES means it must be 6, NO indicates it is 4 or 5; ask if it is 5 - if NO it is 4.

Split the difference in the same way if you got NO to being greater than 3 - it must be between 1 and 3, so check greater than 2, etc.

Third Method - Pointing:

Hold the hand that is NOT holding your Pendulum with the palm open and up. Imagine that the fingers of this hand are numbered 1, 2, 3, 4, and 5 in a clockwise direction - and that going past finger (or thumb) 5 indicates 6.

An alternative schema is to use the spaces before, between, and after your fingers and thumb as indicating the value.

Hold your Pendulum above your open palm, and ask it to point to the finger etc., that indicates the number of spots on the top surface of the dice.

Fourth Method - Awareness:

Some people have the ability to 'move their awareness' around their body - this is not just looking at a part of your body, but imagining that a 'feeling' goes there.

Try to do this, saying *"my left shoulder indicates 1, left hip 2, left foot 3, right foot 4, right hip 5, right shoulder 6"* - make variations if you want !

Then ask your awareness to indicate the number of spots on the top surface of the dice - and 'be aware' of the location of your awareness, the number indicated !

Some people do this using their forehead as a dial - extreme left being 1, with graduations across the top for 2 & 3 on the left side, for 4 & 5 on the right side, and the extreme right side indicating 6.

No scoring here, unless you just want to count how many times that you have success - to see how you are improving your intuitive abilities !

How else can this be used ?

You can assign different values or meanings to different parts of your body, using these as a scale. It is best to keep a constant form to these - and forms to which you are accustomed.

For example, you are probably accustomed to immediately sensing the dials on your car dashboard - clockwise left to right for speed, engine heat, fuel supply; and your charging indicator is central for null, left increasing with discharge (negativity), right increasing with charge (positivity).

So you can assign values or meanings that are pertinent to the situation that you wish to examine, such as health of a patient, chances of success, advisability of an investment, suitability for a purpose, expected response to a proposal.

You can probably think of more examples that concern your own situation, or that of your business, and use them to help make good decisions.

The more that you use this system, the greater grows your confidence in the results obtained.

Lie Detector Game

You need other players, a deck of playing cards, pen/pencil and paper to keep score; you can use any Soul Sense, or a Pendulum.

The object of the game is to use your Intuition to detect if a person is making a true or false statement. The first player who gets 25 points wins the game.

The dealer is the only one who can score points during a round - the players try to keep the dealer from scoring points.

Designate one player to keep score. Then cut for first dealer.

The dealer deals one (1) card to each player (none to him/herself). The player to the left of the dealer starts the game.

This player will choose to tell the dealer either a TRUE or FALSE statement about the value and suit of the card she/be is holding. <u>Example</u>: the player is holding the King of Hearts.

A true statement would be King of Hearts; a false statement would be King of Clubs or 5 of Spades.

The dealer will mentally ask her/his Intuition *"Is this statement true ?"*, and say TRUE or FALSE.

The player's card will be shown - if the dealer answered correctly, the dealer scores one (I) point, otherwise no point is awarded.

Now the dealer moves to the next player and repeats the same sequence. The dealer continues until all players have had their turn, and the dealer adds up all of her/his points and the total is recorded.

The deal is passed on to the player on the left. This starts a new round; the same play sequence is repeated.

Remember the dealer is the only one that can score points.

<u>Simple Variations</u>

You can use 'red or black', the suite name, and/or value - building up to a more complicated game as the players gain confidence.

<u>Betting Variation:</u>

In place of pen and paper, you will need enough poker chips for all the players.

This game is played the same except for betting - the first player will place a bet and the dealer has to match it; the player makes his/her statement about the card they are holding.

If the player fools the dealer, this player wins all the chips. If the dealer is correct, she/he gets the chips.

The dealer moves on the next player and repeats the same process until all players have had a turn. Then the deal moves onto the next player.

The player with the most chips wins.

How else can this be used ?

The ability to tell when you are being told a lie can be used in many different circumstances - a most useful skill ! When you use a Pendulum, it is noticeable by others.

If you develop other signaling methods, such as the blinking of your eye, movement of your tongue, or placement of you awareness (on your forehead as a gauge, or to a body position) then nobody will know !

Nobody can Recall every Book
It Helps to Know just Where to Look

Further Information

About the Author

John Living has been a Royal Engineer, a Chartered Civil Engineer, and a Professional Engineer. He started Dowsing over 50 years ago, being taught as a young officer in the British Army.

John is the Executive Secretary of the Holistic Intuition Society, a member of the American Society of Dowsers, the Canadian Society of Dowsers, and the Canadian Society of Questers.

His articles have been published in the American, British, and Canadian Dowsing society journals.

Holistic Intuition Society

The aims of the Society are to help people to be aware that they have Intuitive abilities, to aid them in developing such skills, and to encourage the use of these for Healing and the general good of 'All that Is'.

The Society's web page at www.in2it.ca has quite a lot of information about Intuition in general and Dowsing in particular - since Dowsing is a very simple method of accessing your Intuition 'On Demand' that can be easily learnt by most people.

John Living is the Executive Secretary of the Society, and may be contacted by email: jliving@direct.ca or telephone:

(250)539-5807 or (Toll Free Canada & USA): 1-866-369-7464

or write to:

John Living, Professional Engineer
RR#1 S9 C6, Galiano Island,
British Columbia, V0N 1P0 Canada

It is advisable to check the Society's web page
for any changes in this information:
www.in2it.ca

Books of Interest

Books are listed: <u>Title</u>, Author(s), *Publisher*, then my comments; note that the books may also be published by other companies.

Books - General Interest

<u>EFT manual</u>, Gary Craig, free download from www.emofree.org

The details of using the 'Emotional Freedom Techniques' as described in the chapter on EFT.

<u>The Secret Life of Plants</u>, Tompkins & Bird, *Avon*

Covers Backster effect, radiance, and much more about plant life that is not known or ignored by the mainstream; understanding plants helps in all aspects of life ! All Peter Tomkins and Chris Bird's books are full of knowledge, well-written, and worth reading - see also <u>Secrets of the Soil</u>.

<u>Anastasia</u>, Vladimir Megre, *www.RingingCedars.com*

Not usually found in bookstores - about the most fascinating account from Siberia of working with 'Upstairs' and nature in a simple but effective way that has changed the life of many Russians - and now others worldwide First of 8 books in a series. Edgar Cayce foretold of a great change originating in Russia - these books could be the cause ! (Ringing Cedars of Russia)

<u>Supernature</u>, Lyall Watson, *Coronet / Hodder & Stoughton*

A biologist looks at life from a metaphysical viewpoint - he outlines and explains aspects that are usually 'papered over' by mainstream scientists. All Lyall's books are most fascinating !

<u>Rebirth of Nature</u>, Rupert Sheldrake, *Bantam Books*

The best book about life and nature from the originator of the concept of a metamorphic field - it enables you to appreciate better how Intuition resonates with reality.

<u>Earth Radiation</u>, Käthe Bachler **See p.165**

Books - Intuitive Abilities

<u>Practical Intuition</u>, Laura Day, *Vermillion - Random House*

An excellent book explaining how to develop your Intuition, with many examples. Also see her other good books: 'The Circle', 'Practical Intuition for Success', 'Practical Intuition for Love', published by Harper Collins or Penguin Putnam.

Psychic Discoveries behind the Iron Curtain,   Ostrander & Schroeder, *Bantam*

".. This book has nothing to do with 'psychic' anything - but 'Matters that we have been taught to _call_ psychic !'"

A wonderful look at the way that the old Soviet Union showed interest in investigating the non-physical dimension, including Kirlian photography.

Lessons in ESP, David St Clair, *Signet*

A real 'Do it Yourself' guide to many aspects of developing and using your 'psychic' abilities' - easy to read, simple instructions that can be followed to improve your life.

Urban Shaman, Serge Kahili King, *Fireside / Simon & Schuster*

Based on Huna know-how from Hawaii - how to use shamanic methods to improve life for yourself and your family. See also his Kahuna Healing, *Quest Books*.

You are Psychic !, Pete A. Sanders, Jr., *Fawcett Columbine*

Without any doubt, the very best book that I have ever read on understanding and developing your 'Soul Senses' - which is called 'being psychic'. I have found this to be a great help in all that I do - and especially with relationships at home and at work.

See also his Access your Brain's Joy Centre, *www.FreeSoul.net*

Books - Using Intuitive Tools

Intuition Technology, John Living, **See p.167**

Elements of Pendulum Dowsing, Tom Graves, *Element*

Excellent easy to read - and amusing - book, covers games, map Dowsing, and much more; it even covers finding bugs in computer programs!

Pendulum Workbook, Markus Schirner, *Sterling Publishing*

Basic facts about Pendulums, exceptionally good introduction to using charts for health - beautifully prepared book, with super illustrations of many charts which can be used to identify the causes of health problems and indicate solutions.

Universal Allergy Healing Charts, Juanita Ott & Dora Sharpe

Visit www.Mirrorwaters.com for this and their other chart books.

Books - More Advanced Healing

Energy Medicine, Donna Eden, *Penguin / Putnam*

Many techniques that you can use to Heal yourself and others, to reduce pain and remove illness using 'Hands Off' techniques - a 'Best Value' for Healing.

DreamHealer, Adam, *Penguin* *www.DreamHealer.com*

A young Canadian has the ability to help other people Heal - and guides you in how to Heal yourself, mainly using belief and visualization. See also DreamHealer 2 & 3. DVD is also available.

Kundalini and the Chakras, Genevieve Paulson, *Llewellyn*

So many people suffer strange illnesses caused by their Kundalini system 'opening up' - and most medical doctors are completely at a loss to help, since they do not understand the causes ! An outstanding book on explaining how the energy body operates.

Hands of Light, Barbara Ann Brennan, *Bantam Books*

Excellent book telling how she sees people's energy bodies, and using this knowledge for Healing . See also Light Emerging.

Essential Reiki, Diane Stein, *Crossing Press*

A very thorough introduction to Reiki, with full explanations - now there is no need to pay for expensive initiation by self-professed masters ! Learn the skills, then practice - get experience with other Reiki Healers as well for best results.

Awakening the Third Eye, Samuel Sagan, MD, *Clairvision*

Dr Samuel Sagan has an Indo-French-Anglo-Digger background, and he combines this with Chinese Healing and mystical understanding to develop new vistas of Healing. Techniques sound simple, but are not anywhere as simple as those previously mentioned - but may be more easy if you are already have some clairvoyant abilities. Fascinating reading !

Some Interesting Web Sites

Nexus New Times Magazine: www.nexusmagazine.com
Sanjeevini Healing Cards: www.saisanjeevini.org
Emotional Freedom Techniques: www.emofree.com
Dr Masaru Emoto Water Crystals: www.thank-water.net/english
life-enthusiast.com/twilight/research_emoto.htm & www.hado.net
'Number One Allergy Detective'   www.scott-mumby.com

Earth Radiation - Käthe Bachler

2nd English Edition, with a commentary by John Living

This is the classic record of the identification and location of energies from the earth which are noxious to human beings.

The book is a distillation of over 11,000 cases of investigation of these energies in more than 3,000 homes in 14 countries !

Originally written in German, it became a 'best seller' in Europe and was translated first into Spanish, and then into English. The first English edition has long been 'out of print', and existing second hand copies have been fetching prices of US$90 on eBay !

Illustrations show the location of 'Curry Grid Lines' and 'Noxious Water Veins' that radiate noxious energies, especially where they cross.

These illustrations are accompanied by records of the illnesses resulting from sleeping or sitting for a long time in the energy fields - and how great improvements in health occurred when the location of beds, school seats, etc., were moved.

Very simple, very cheap, and very effective !

"We do not claim that every zone of disturbance will result in cancer. Rather, we have found zones of disturbance in every case of cancer. ... Physicians ought to consider geopathic influences as one possible cause of illness, and recommend moving the bed on a trial basis"

Many other illnesses have also been observed to result from these noxious energies - pregnancy failures, infant mortality, insomnia, inattention at school, improper behaviour, rheumatism, multiple sclerosis, parasitic attacks, and more.

Case# 660. The ten-month-old baby was tied to his crib.

The parents were afraid he might fall out of bed, because he stood up again and again.

When in his playpen, he only occupied the half which was "free of radiation," never the half above the curry strip. The father finally phoned me:

"Since we moved the bed, we have had no problem with his sleeping and he is healthy and robust."

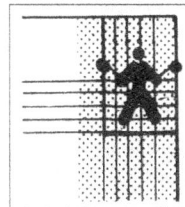

<u>Case# 403. She had a crying spell almost every day.</u>

She and two other children had their desks moved, and the symptoms of all three children disappeared

(principal's confirmation available.)

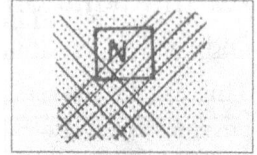

Many of the results are attested by medical doctors who found that cures were only effective after exposure to noxious earth energies ceased. Cases are quoted which include the use of these techniques by physicians for their own health.

<u>Case# 1367. Physician Dr H required a gall bladder operation.</u>

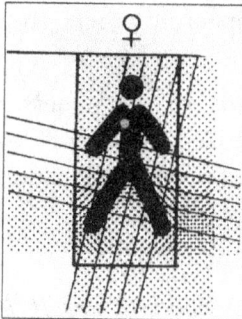

Ever since she moved to her present sleeping place she had been ill.

She suffered from pain and anxiety attacks at night in bed.

Everywhere else she seemed to sleep well.

She changed the bed immediately - and slept better the very first night.

She said: *"I don't understand why conventional medicine does not acknowledge the value of dowsing. It seems to me they ought to be grateful for the help."*

One of the key points that this book makes is that many other problems, not just cancer, are attributable to some large degree to earth energies that are noxious to humans.

By eliminating the effects of these we can expect improvements in education and in behaviour, reductions in work losses and medical expenses, and better health at minimal cost.

<u>Case# 1486c. A chemist from Salzburg</u>

felt discomfort, registered slight fevers, and was nervous while working at his bench in his laboratory.

Many of his experiments failed and had to be repeated.

Whenever he worked at a place free of radiation, his experiments proved to be successful.

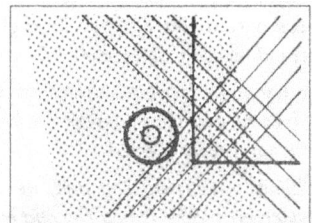

Intuition Technology

John originally wrote a text book for a weekend course called 'Intuition Technology - The Users Manual and Certificate Course' designed for teaching Dowsing; the appendices included important information that could not be covered in just one weekend - hundreds of copies have been sold, with much positive feed-back - and not one complaint !

This book, Intuition 'On Demand', covers some of that course. The new book, 'Intuition Technology', includes most of the work in this book and in the Users Manual, plus a greatly expanded discussion on 'who we are', examination of our energy bodies, and how we can Heal the energies that cause us health problems and so achieve good health - without the side effects often resulting from medicinal drugs.

The essential 'stuff' of these books is that we all have Intuition, and our Heart-Mind-Brain team provides the best linkage to our Intuition - giving signals via our nervous-muscular system.

The skills taught in this book have been used for a great many years - mainly to help others. There are many wonderful teachers around the globe, and this book tries to collect their wisdom together. Even experienced Dowsers will gain from reading this book - since some aspects have not previously been explained in simple terms.

Aspects of Dowsing that are included: locating water wells and minerals; finding lost items and hidden objects such as land mines; accessing information from the 'Universal Knowledge Banks'; locating noxious energies and Healing them; identifying health problems and finding ways to overcome them; and improving the well-ness of people by using our 'Power of Thought' assisted by paper 'Radionics Machines'.

Everything that exists is made of energy - and this applies to other dimensions as well as the physical dimensions. Knowing this, we can understand how to work with 'All That Is' for the general good.

The techniques taught in this book cannot hurt anyone - but can help people to create a better and more healthy life, for themselves and for others !

Miracles do happen when we work with 'Upstairs' having the intent of helping others with 'True Holy Love'.

English Speaking Dowsing Organizations

See www.in2it.ca for current addresses and internet connections.

Australia

Dowsers Society of NS Wales
7 Maycock St, Denistone East, NSW
  www.divstrat.com.au
  dsnsw@yahoo.com.au

Dowsing Society of Victoria
Box 2635, Mount Waverley, VIC 3149
  www.dsv.org.au

Dowsers' Club of S Australia Inc
9 Mersey Court, Para Hills,
South Australia 5096.

North Tasmania Dowsing Association
2515 West Tamar Highway, Exeter,
Tasmania 7275, Australia.

South Tasmania Dowsing Association
PO Box 530, Moonah, Tasmania 7009,

Canada

Canadian Society of Dowsers
(Ontario and eastern Canada)
487 Lynden Rd RR#8,
Brantford , ON N3T 5M1
  www.canadiandowsers.org
  1-888-588-8958

Canadian Society of Questers
(Prairies and British Columbia)
POBox 4873, Vancouver, BC V6B 4A6
  www.questers.ca
  (604) 944-8683

Ireland

Society of Irish Dowsers
31 Ardmore Grove, Artane, Dublin 5
  www.irishdiviners.com

New Zealand

NZ Society of Dowsing and Radionics
PO Box 41-095, St Luke's,
Mt. Albert, Auckland 1030, NZ
  www.dowsingnewzealand.org
  jackiedow@paradise.net.nz

United Kingdom

British Society of Dowsers
2 St. Ann's Road, Malvern,
Worcestershire, WR14 4RG
  www.britishdowsers.org
  44 01624 576969
  info@britishdowsers.org

United States of America

American Society of Dowsers
P.O. Box 24, Danville,
VT 05828-0024, USA
  www.dowsers.org
  (802) 684-3417
  asd@dowsers.org

Ozark Research Institute
PO Box 387, Fayetteville,
AR 72702-0387
  www.ozarkresearch.org
  (479) 582-9197

Email Lists open to all who are interested in Dowsing

International Society of Dowsers
Purely web based - www.internationaldowsers.org
To join, go to: www.groups.yahoo.com/group/digital-dowsers/join
(Note: a Yahoo! ID is required)
Or email: digital-dowsers-subscribe@yahoogroups.com - no message needed.

ASD Digital Dowsers
is an online cyber chapter of ASD meeting round the clock, planet wide.
To join, see: www.photon.cc/mailman/listinfo/digitaldowsers
Membership of American Society of Dowsers is NOT required !

The Holistic Intuition Society's 'Shop'

DVDs of Speakers and Workshops

We have recorded the lectures and workshops on Dowsing and on Healing at the conventions promoted by the Society, and have these available on DVDs that are playable world-wide. See **www.in2it.ca/videos.htm** for details

The workshops were given by recognized masters of Dowsing to teach their skills - including the ability of Dowsers to use their 'Power of Thought' for healing the energies of humans, animals, and plants.

"Love Living" Bracelets

Background

In the 1925 Georges Lakhovsky in France developed a coil for the protection of trees; copper wire was stuck into the ground, turns were made around the tree, and the loose end was pointed towards the sky as an aerial. In 1928 he formed a variation of this that was geared to improve the health of humans, which he called the 'multi-wave oscillator', based on his then new theory that cells are microscopic oscillating circuits.

This was successfully used in French, Italian, and Swedish clinics, and when Lakhovsky escaped to the USA in 1941 it proved successful in a major New York hospital. Among problems successfully treated were cancerous growths from Radium burns, goiters, arthritis, chronic bronchitis, congenital hip dislocation, and many others. (Tompkins & Bird: 'Secret Life of Plants').

Design of the Rings

John Living made a number of different rings, testing the effect on glasses of water showed that the water had a radiance of about 5KÅ (5,000 Ångstroms - the human body for a normal person is about 6.5 KÅ) which in 2 minutes increased to 20KÅ for the medium sized rings and 60 KÅ for the smallest ring - the effect is more concentrated.

They are sturdy, attractive, and within the reach of most purses. So which ring type is best ? This depends on the use !

The bracelets and smaller rings #1, #2, and #3 are of twisted copper wire, having a small gap; a vinyl tube prevents the copper from being in direct contact with your skin.

They give your blood the vibrational pattern of copper, similar to the way a homeopathic remedy works.

This waterproof casing design permits easy cleaning, prevents corrosion, and allows opening.

These rings can be worn, or used to energize foods and drinks. The medium ring, #6, is similar - it fits on most chairs for you to sit on.

The larger rings, #8, #10, and #12, are of 1/4 inch diameter copper tube (for increased sturdiness) having a twisted wire connector in the gap to encourage clockwise rotation of the energies in the tube.

They are intended for healing the energies in a body and in its aura.

The vinyl encased copper bracelet is sealed watertight, for easy washing, and the combination of vinyl with copper blends into the skin colour, so that the bracelet is less noticeable. A hardy bracelet, suitable for constant wear, even ideal for a man in the office or working outside.

Using the Rings

The strongest effect is in the plane of the ring. It seems that 'not good' energies cannot exist inside the ring; the effect is also 'transmitted' in a column above and below this plane, expanding at 45° and reducing in intensity as the distance increases.

To find which size LOVE LIVING bracelet fits you:

Measure around your ankle / wrist with a tape measure send it to us, and we will send you the size just greater than your measurement.

Wear your bracelet loosely - leave about 1/2 to 1 inch gap between the ends.

You can expect all the water in your body (over 75% of you !) to become potentized with a high radiance.

Germs and viruses do not thrive in such an environment, so your LOVE LIVING Bracelets helps to keep you healthy !

A number of successes are reported with the relief of headaches by placing a #2 Energy ring around the neck - if below a shirt or sweater, it is not noticeable.

It may be that some people who have other head problems, perhaps including Alzheimer's and Parkinson's diseases, benefit from wearing a neck ring. The cost of a trial is minimal, the possible benefits considerable, and there is no health risk involved .

A Simple Test you can do yourself

Put water from the same source into 2 glasses and put one glass into your 'LOVE LIVING' Energy Ring. After 10 minutes taste each glass. Repeat at 20 minutes and 30 minutes.

You can expect the untreated water to retain its original taste, while the taste of the treated water improves.

At the same time you can use an Aurameter (or other Dowsing tool) to check the location of the aura of the water; you will find that the aura of the treated water expands !

'L' Rods

These are made from welding rods, with a wooden handle having a plastic insert for low friction movement and a metal end cap.

The rod arm has a metal end cap to enhance your Dowsing response and prevent damage to people.

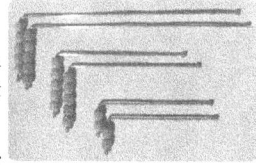

Glass Bead Pendulums

The glass beads have been hand made by craftsmen, and come in various colours and configurations; they are held by a braided nylon string, the string colour being suitable for the bead.

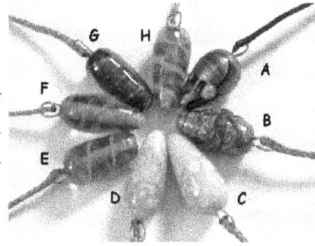

Bendable Bobber

This tool has pewter weights fitted to the end of a specially wound spring 'wand' inserted into a ball-point pen case. It give great sensitivity, and bends to fit in your pocket.

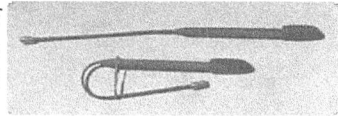

More Information

The Holistic Intuition Society sells more Dowsing and Healing tools - these are shown on our website at: **www.in2it.ca/tools.htm**   together with prices and ordering information.

The key intent is to provide simple tools that can be easily used, at reasonable cost, and that do their job effectively and safely without any side effects.

The Holistic Intuition Society

c/o Executive Secretary: John Living, Professional Engineer
RR# 1 S9 C6,   Galiano Island,   BC,   V0N 1P0   Canada
Telephone (250)539-5807   Toll Free Canada & USA: 1-866-369-7464

**Unfortunately we cannot process credit cards - except by PayPal
PayPal is set-up on our web site,
A cheque or money order in Canadian or US funds is acceptable.**

www.ingramcontent.com/pod-product-compliance
Lightning Source LLC
Chambersburg PA
CBHW072249270326
41930CB00010B/2324